DARK SKIES

TALES OF TURBULENCE IN PARADISE

DAVID HALDANE

Black Rose Writing | Texas

The author grants the final approval for this literary material.

First printing

Some names and identifying details may have been changed to protect the privacy of individuals

ISBN: 978-1-68513-596-6
PUBLISHED BY BLACK ROSE WRITING
www.blackrosewriting.com

Printed in the United States of America
Suggested Retail Price (SRP) $19.95

Dark Skies is printed in Georgia Pro

*As a planet-friendly publisher, Black Rose Writing does its best to eliminate unnecessary waste to reduce paper usage and energy costs, while never compromising the reading experience. As a result, the final word count vs. page count may not meet common expectations.

PRAISE FOR HALDANE'S WORK

"Haldane's storytelling is rapid, fast-paced, devoid of filler (and) heavy on action."
–Long Beach Press Telegram

"Instead of exoticizing things he does not fully understand, he tries to actually understand them...Haldane's descriptions can be a source of social history."
–Manila Times

"...a series of light personal essays...some of them hilarious, others refreshingly tender."
–Manila Bulletin

"Haldane's work expresses the joy of living a full life and meditating seriously upon it."
–Ron Featheringill, PhD, author of *The Tension Between Divine Will and Human Free Will in Milton and the Classical Epic Tradition.*

"Haldane is a deliberate writer, framing each short chapter in a lesson, a realization, an `aha' moment...The short chapters are often poignant."
–Philippine Star

"David writes like a dream."
–Marcel L. Milliam, author of *Human (is) Nature: A Year in Haiku*

To my beloved brother, Kenneth Haldane,
who got there before me.

These are essays of resilience.

The idea of moving to the Philippines was borne of desperation. Life in America had changed for my Filipino wife, Ivy, and me; what had once been easy had become exceedingly difficult. And so we pulled up our roots and built a new home in the place of her birth.

My 2023 collection, *A Tooth in My Popsicle and Other Ebullient Essays on Becoming Filipino*, tells the story of our first two years in Northern Mindanao. It is, at heart, a love story about adapting to a new culture and way of life different from anything I'd ever known.

This book describes what happened after that. It tells of our temporary escape from the world's strictest COVID lockdown, wherein borders were shut and schools darkly shuttered. It portrays the horrific Category Five super typhoon that nearly destroyed our seaside dream house and everything in it. And it testifies to the alarming surge of antisemitism and other problems in a world and country I never thought they would reach.

Interspersed are sections describing the Philippines' eternal and almost mystical land and sea. And, of course, a section pertaining to the island nation's colorful and startling culture that continues to fascinate not only me, but most foreigners who traverse these beautiful shores.

Mostly, though, it's a book about coping.

As with the earlier book, the bulk of these essays appeared originally as columns in the *Mindanao Gold Star Daily* which published them exclusively for over five years. Others appeared in *The Manila Times*, where that weekly column now resides.

The overarching theme is survival and recovery, outcomes for which I am grateful and proud.

–David Haldane
Surigao City, Philippines
April 2025

DARK SKIES

PROLOGUE
DARK SKIES

It was like stepping into a surreal world under a dark cloud of gloom. Exiting the terminal at Los Angeles International Airport, I couldn't help but notice the ethereal haze hanging over everything like a moldy yellow blanket. "Wow, I haven't seen this much smog in years," I told my wife, recalling the overcast days of my childhood when we were forced to stay inside. Then I remembered what I'd been reading before leaving the Philippines, that this was the worst wildfire season in California history. Ah, not smog but *smoke*, I realized with an involuntary shudder. And suddenly I found myself in a world that was strangely familiar yet unnervingly different. Much like the one we had just left behind.

We'd been in the Philippines for more than two years when the pandemic struck. The house we built overlooking Surigao Strait had barely been finished when ominous microscopic organisms began attacking the earth. Almost overnight, it seemed, the strange became familiar, and the familiar became strange.

We stuck it out as long as we could, and probably would have stayed forever. But now we had children, and their needs became paramount. Amid what's been called the world's strictest lockdown, Philippine schools had been closed for nearly our entire stay. And so the country's students—among them our dear son—had been forced to endure what we euphemistically referred to as "online learning."

That was happening everywhere, of course. While the Philippines stayed closed, however, the loud complaints of parents in the United States signaled a possible change. So we returned to the land we had left, hoping that things would be different.

Wildfires are nothing new in Southern California. Almost every year, for as long as anyone can remember, they've inflamed the hillsides in the hot summer months. Ecologists view the annual burnings as part of a natural cycle. Once they were kept in check with controlled burnings performed regularly by firefighters. Growing up, I frequently saw the smoke of those burns rising from the fields alongside the freeways. These days, though, pressure from environmentalists has made that smoke rare.

"We dug ourselves into a dangerous fuel imbalance," award-winning environmental reporter Elizabeth Weil has written. "We live in a Mediterranean climate that's designed to burn" yet don't allow that burn to occur.This year's wildfires are more catastrophic than most. Breathing the smoke-filled air, one resident told the *Washington Post*, is "like sticking yourself in a little room with 12 people around you smoking cigarettes." The psychological effects may be even worse. It's the pain "experienced when there's recognition that the place where one resides is under immediate attack," Australian environmental philosopher Glenn Albrecht has postulated. He calls the malaise *solastalgia*, a combination of nostalgia, solace and desolation, i.e. "the erosion of a sense of belonging to a particular place" and "a feeling of distress about its transformation." It's a form of homesickness one gets, he says, "when one is still home."

Not unlike how we felt in the Philippines. Our fondest hope is that one day soon, that island nation will be again feel like home.

1.
THE LAND AND THE SEA

ON GOD'S ORDERS: THE ERUPTION OF MT. PINATUBO

It was almost Biblical.

First came the earthquake, one of the most powerful the Philippines had ever seen. Then, almost simultaneously, Typhoon Diding and the eruption of Mount Pinatubo killed more than 800 people, wiping out Luzon's Clark Air Base. And finally, just three months later, came the coup de grâce; the Philippine Senate sent the US military packing after a presence of almost 90 years.

"I think of it every day," Mark R. Clifford, 59, says of the June 15, 1991, volcanic eruption that just turned 33. "It's the kind of experience that makes you believe in life after death."

Back then, Clifford was a 26-year-old US Marine from San Francisco, California, stationed near Subic Bay to provide protection from the communist National People's Army. Suddenly, on Philippine Independence Day, a superior officer called to alert him and the 19 marines he was commanding of an impending danger.

"It wasn't on my radar at all," Clifford recalls. "I looked up and saw this huge white cloud like somebody had spilled milk across the blue tropical sky." Before long, he says, "ash was covering our uniforms and we could barely breathe."

When the major eruption finally happened a few days later, Clifford and his men were huddled safely inside a Quonset hut -

a small, metal shelter. "The eruption turned the sky black for more than 24 hours," he remembers. "The ash was so heavy it defoliated the surrounding jungle. We were being buried alive, preparing for death, and we knew it."

Despite being a brash young man sequestered with others of the same ilk, Clifford prayed. "It was like sitting atop the gallows," he recalls, "just riding out the blackness. I remember lying on my rack, thinking of my fiancé back home, who I thought would never see me again. Then it stopped."

Glad to be alive, the men dug their way out through the hot ash, singeing their fingers as they did. Then remained in the Philippines for several weeks more to help Filipinos deal with the aftermath.

Clifford eventually left the military, returned to Northern California, married the fiancé whose image had sustained him, enjoyed a long career in law enforcement, and raised two boys and a girl. But he never forgot that day of darkness in the Philippines.

"I died in that Quonset hut," he told me shortly before the anniversary of the cataclysmic event that shaped the country's future. "When you have lots of time to review your life, it causes a spiritual awakening. Sleeping peacefully, I believed I would never wake up."

In 2020, the same year he retired as a police sergeant, Clifford published *Typhoon Coast,* a novel inspired by his near-death experience in the shadow of Mt. Pinatubo. "There is a mix of magic and mystery that...hold [s] the story together," one reviewer wrote. The book "is an excellent psychological journey."

Later, the budding novelist described the experience further in a published short story. "Pinatubo's eruption brings darkness as we trudge through the streets of Olongapo," Clifford wrote. "Olongapo is why God invented purgatory. Under the volcano's gauntlet, I hear Tagalog cries and shouts. I imagine they are prayers for help, wishes for death. Silent was the music that blared from bustling strip bars. The ash is too thick to smell the wafts of sewage that once mixed with the barbecue smoke...The jungle cracks under the weight of Pinatubo's eruption."

Clifford has never returned to the Philippines, a situation he intends to soon remedy. "I have to go back," he says. "It's a non-issue, I don't have a choice."

One of his primary goals is to scale Mt. Pinatubo. "It will finally give me some closure," the former Marine explains.

Just as it did for the Philippines so many decades ago.

THE DEATH OF A TREE

Though I never touched it, my children have swung from its branches. And hearing their laughter always gave me great joy.

I'm referring to the famed "Coconut Bent Tree" overhanging the Maasin River in Pilar, my wife's hometown on Siargao Island. For years, it provided succor and entertainment for both tourists and locals. Now it's gone, apparently brought down by that heavy burden.

"It is with great sadness [we announce] the well-known [tree] has reached its end," Pilar's department of Tourism, Culture and Arts said in a social media post. "Pilar is thankful for the resources given by the Almighty... to preserve the 'Coconut Bent Tree' that... gave livelihood to the community."

In a separate post, a group called Litik Maasin River-Siargao addressed the former shrub directly. "Everything has a limit," it said. "Thank you for the time you were here with us, for helping each of us... We will try to continue what you started. We will miss you so much Coconut bent tree."

No one knows exactly how or when the tree's unique abilities first came to light. I have no memories of it from my earliest visits to Siargao in 2006. But as the island attracted more and more tourists seeking adventure, the tree became a familiar fixture. Visitors would act as little Tarzans, dangling from its branches overhanging the water.

"Nothing lasts forever," photographer Janos Andanar re-captioned a 2018 photo. "Good thing I took a picture... before it became famous."

The hanging coconut tree had miraculously survived major typhoons that devastated the island, causing billions of pesos in damage. Among the weather's casualties were the renowned Cloud 9 pier on which I proposed to my wife. But the tree bent over the Maasin River had always stood firm, playing a critical role in the island's survival and resurgence by attracting and entertaining gushes of returning tourists.

It may have been that exertion that finally caused its demise.

The famous tree's death, a local cultural organization called Lokal Lab Siargao declared, is a "wake-up call" regarding development. Tourists, the group said in a post, must "be more responsible. We learned that there was a no-climbing sign put on the tree recently, yet... some tourists continued to climb."

The irony, of course, is that any enforced climbing restrictions would have considerably diminished the tree's vaunted tourist appeal. And therein lies the rub, the eternal tension between tourism's economic benefits and its potential environmental cost.

Ivy and I had our own tussle with that tension back in 2018. It happened at Magpupungko Beach, not far from the notorious bent tree, where she and her family own property. All her life, Ivy has dreamed of building a modest resort on the 7000-plus-square-meter beachfront lot now titled in her name. And as the swarms of tourists began arriving, we figured it was time.

But to build a cabin, we had to remove trees. Specifically, six coconut trees that had long provided shade, beauty, and, occasionally, the refreshing taste of buko juice sipped from the shell.

Those trees meant everything to me. Though we had been convinced of the necessity of removing them, neither Ivy nor I realized how hard it would be. We found out one morning, as the eager crew of tree cutters arrived to do its work. For a while, I watched with a sinking heart as those loyal, long-serving trees fell. Then retreated to a nearby porch to grieve. Finally, Ivy, unable to watch any longer, came and sat down beside me. With tears in our eyes, we hugged each other and promised to cut no more trees.

My point is simply this: I understand the pain at Maasin River.

DIVING IN THE PHILIPPINES

I used to live underwater.

Well, ok, maybe that's an exaggeration; let's just say I used to spend my weekends and vacations there. And what wonderful weekends they were!

Those memorable hours included swimming in the clear waters of Hawaii, spearfishing in Baja, drift diving in Cozumel, and cave diving in Cayman. Some of them were also spent navigating the underwater caverns of Akumal, the sand falls of Cabo, the luscious kelp beds and shipwrecks of Southern California, and the fiery soft corals of Fiji Island.

Once I spent several days exploring Australia's Great Barrier Reef. And another time I actually spent the night in an underwater hotel off Florida's Key Largo, accessible only with scuba.

By the time I got to the Philippines, I was all dived out. Or so I thought.

But then my adult daughter, Adina, reminded me of something I had promised her as a child. "Dad," she said during a visit to Mindanao, "you always told me someday you'd take me diving. Let's do it now!"

And so we did.

A friend named Jake Miranda—a retired Philippine Navy diver—ran a dive center in Surigao City at a place called Punta

Bilar. Because Adina had never been diving and I hadn't been diving in years, he gave us both an introductory lesson. Then, using rented gear, we dipped into the tropical waters of Surigao Strait.

The familiar feeling of weightless wonder enveloped me like a winsome wave. Everywhere the coral called, and the fish beckoned from a reef they call House. It was as beautiful as anything I'd ever seen.

Drifting over the sand, the miraculous wonder I hadn't gazed upon in ages still felt ingrained in my bones and soul, like a soothing dream. Along with the dream came a strong current pushing gently against our skin.

Jake had warned us about it. "Just go with the flow," he'd said. "Don't fight it, just relax and let it take you where it will."

So that's what we did. The water moved us as if in flight, whisking the shimmering scenery of the ocean floor past us far below. Suddenly, we were moving quickly. And then we weren't, as Jake slowly led us ashore.

That's when something prophetic happened that we wouldn't recognize for years; the place we emerged was almost the exact spot whereupon we later built the house in which I now sit writing these words.

Here's the good news: In 2023, it seems, visiting divers poured over a billion dollars into the Philippine economy. "As one of the most mega biodiverse countries in the world, we are home to more than 500 species of corals and 2,000 species of fish," Tourism Secretary Christina Garcia Frasco said at the opening ceremonies of that year's Philippine International Dive Expo in Manila. The distinction, she continued, "is something we take to heart."

Back in Surigao City, meanwhile, I often sit on the veranda of my house, gazing wistfully over the reef of the same name.

Jake Miranda's dive center closed long ago, and the underwater gear I shipped here from California lies gathering dust in the basement.

My favorite fantasy? That one day, God willing, I shall again glide over the bountiful reef they call House.

FISHING

It wasn't my first time.

As a child, my father used to take me fishing in gurgling mountain streams. Later, I took my own two children—now grown—on ocean excursions for fun. So accepting my Canadian friend Gordon's offer of two days aboard a chartered fish boat off Siargao Island wasn't a bridge very far.

"It'll be great!" he promised. "It'll be good for your son."

Gordon was speaking of Isaac, then 12, who'd never fished in his life. And so on a recent Sunday, Isaac, Ivy, and I arose early to spend the day combing the ocean for food.

It started like most journeys off Siargao's luscious coast; surrounded by a crystalline blue sea, we felt the sun on our backs and the breeze at our breasts as the nylon lines dangled expectantly behind. Then came the wait. Which seemed to stretch out forever. Until the sun grew oppressive and the surge became a dirge.

Being aboard a 32-foot fiberglass monohull doesn't leave much space for shade. So we three relaxed in the back, while Gordon and his girlfriend eagerly awaiting the day's first catch at the bow.

That's when Ivy threw up.

"Oh," she moaned. "I don't feel so good."

"Try to heave overboard," I suggested, helping her lean over the side while holding back her gorgeous long black hair. And so she did, splattering the ocean with the unappealing contents of her gut. Then she sank to the deck, where she spent the rest of the day.

Next came Isaac's turn. "Hey dad," he inquired weakly, "do you think we could make a quick stop to drop me off?"

I shrugged. "We're pretty far out to sea," I said, "so it's not very likely."

"I'm panicking," Isaac announced. "My heart's beating fast!"

Once again, I made a beeline for the starboard side, this time with my son in tow. "Look at the horizon," I urged, gently massaging his back. "Think of nice things. Tell me about the games you like to play."

Isaac spent the next 15 minutes describing, with increasing confidence, his favorite games on X-box, including *Call of Duty* and *World War Z.* As he spoke, I felt his heartbeat miraculously slow.

I understood his pain, having earlier experienced a momentary panic myself. It happened as I lay resting in the sun, thankfully protected by sunscreen as thick as a shirt, when it suddenly dawned on me that there was no way out. No matter how rough the sea got, how hot the sun burned, or how hard nausea pushed on our insides, we were there for the duration. Which promised to be a very long time.

And it occurred to me then how much fishing resembles life. We endure hours of boredom, discomfort, panic, pain, and for what? A few moments of triumphant pleasure that may never come.

It certainly didn't arrive on that day. "I think the fish took a vacation," I told the boatman on the dock following eight hours of misery. "Apparently, even *they* need time off."

Unbowed, Gordon and his mate vowed to return the following day and try their luck anew, an opportunity we politely declined. Sure enough, the next day they bagged a beautiful eight-foot Blue Marlin sailfish weighing more than 66 pounds.

Seeing the delicious catch, we quickly demanded our unearned share. Like I said, fishing is a lot like life.

THE SEA GYPSIES COME ASHORE

The joke made me cringe.

"Are you a goodjau or a Badjau?" my companion asked the pretty young girl standing in the parking lot with an outstretched hand.

To my utter astonishment, she shot us a gamely grin. "I'm a goodjau," she said. Apparently, she had heard the joke before. And so we gave her all our spare change.

In Northern Mindanao where I live, the Sama-Badjau (also spelled Bajau or Bajo) are ubiquitous. You see them everywhere, but especially in the parking lots of restaurants and malls or strolling along the seaside boulevard where they're sure to catch a crowd. Easily identified by their distinctive yellow, red, gold, and black native garb, they are almost always young, female, and begging for money.

Sometimes they carry babies or are surrounded by small children pressing fingers to their lips in a universal gesture of hunger. But always they look forlorn, piercing the hearts of passersby with beseeching looks that are hard to deny.

It wasn't always so.

The first time I saw these colorful indigenous people was nearly two decades ago off the coast of southern Mindanao's Zamboanga City, and oh, what a difference! They lived in boats with sails the same bright colors as their garb. A nomadic tribe subsisting mainly on fishing, the women would come ashore only occasionally to sell the colorful weavings for which they were famous. Once I bought one that, for many years, decorated a wall of my Southern California home.

But, alas, things have changed for these so-called “sea gypsies.” It began as early as 1915 when ruling American colonialists dissolved the Sultanate of Sulu, a Sunni Muslim state that, for five centuries, had acted as the Bajau’s patron. More recently, these gentle souls have experienced discrimination and even violence at the hands of the region’s majority Tausug people, most of whom share their Muslim faith but consider them uncivilized outsiders.

And so a great number of the country’s estimated 500,000 Bajaus, hoping for better lives, have migrated north to Palawan, the Visayas, southern Luzon and, yes, my own Surigao City. The problem is that they left their boats behind. And so, strangers in a strange new place, many must now beg on the streets or rely on government subsidies just to get by.

“To those who study the Bajo, there’s little question the culture is increasingly assimilating to life on land and losing touch with its nomadic, seafaring past,” the *New York Times* reported in a recent article entitled “Seafaring Nomads Settle Down Without Quite Embracing Life on Land.”

Focusing mostly on Indonesia—home to the world’s third largest Bajau population behind the Philippines’ largest—the article quotes a researcher in Thailand regarding the group’s changing culture. “The Bajo we see today are not the Bajo that we used to know,” Wengki Ariando, a researcher at Bangkok’s Chulalongkorn University, told the newspaper. The sad thing, he said, is that “they have lost their identity.”

And yet some vestiges of it remain.

The first Bajaus I ever saw in Surigao, actually, were young boys swimming alongside my ferryboat as it arrived from Cebu. Their game: begging delighted passengers to throw coins, for which they would dive using homemade masks and fins.

Whether consciously or not, those young divers were mimicking an important part of traditional Bajau culture, namely free diving with spearguns for fish. In fact, the Bajau became so adept at it over the centuries that they are believed to be endowed with enhancing genetic adaptations such as enlarged spleens, allowing them to extend their dives.

So what does all this mean to an old landlubber like me?

Just that the next time I see a Bajau with her hand out, I'll think twice before turning away. And secretly pray that somehow these beautiful people will one day find their way.

IMMORTALITY

I had no idea we were swimming with saviors.

It was 2006, and I was in the Philippines meeting my future wife. Being a thoughtful hostess, she treated me to a tour of Bucas Grande Island, a hidden gem of Northern Mindanao in the province we now inhabit. And there, tucked away in that natural wonderland, was the little-known stingless jellyfish sanctuary of Tojoman Lagoon.

My God, I thought, slipping into the ocean from the paddleboat we had rented. They were everywhere; swarms of swirling, stunning, see-through spheres rubbing against us with seeming affection. *Oh my God*, I repeated to myself in awed wonder. *I've never seen anything like this*.

What I didn't know then is that they were also immortal. That information came to me via a recent *Wall Street Journal* article about a team of Spanish scientists mapping the genetic code of a jellyfish known for its ability to be literally recreate itself.

"Dubbed the immortal jellyfish," the paper reports, "the tiny sea creature can turn its biological clock backward and revert to a clump of juvenile cells..." When the going gets tough, in other words, they simply get reborn.

Having just celebrated my 74th birthday, I must admit to a certain interest in this subject. It recently came up, in fact, during a telephone conversation with my 38-year-old daughter.

"Dad," she said, "I have to ask you a question, and I hope you won't get mad." It seems her mother-in-law—slightly older than me—had undergone a near fatal heart surgery that raised uncomfortable questions. "So I was wondering," my daughter went on cautiously, "whether, when you die, you'll leave anything to me or only to your *other* family?"

Meaning, of course, my more recent Filipino one.

The question is more complicated than meets the eye because, while my oldest daughter is nearing 40, my youngest isn't yet three. Not to mention a 12-year-old son whose mother is only slightly older than the daughter asking questions.

"Of course I will," I quickly assured her. "We just need to figure out the details."

In fact, I intend to walk my youngest daughter down the aisle on her wedding day. Or, more likely, have her push me down it in a wheelchair. Either way, I'm not planning to die anytime soon.

Ah, but recent headlines have called that assumption into question. Life expectancy in the United States, it seems, has experienced a precipitous decline. While the average American lived to 79 in 2019, according to the *New York Times*, that dipped to 76 in 2021. The drop was "historic," one expert told the paper, attributing it to COVID and other factors including a rise in accidental deaths and drug overdoses.

But, hey, I don't live in the US anymore, so perhaps that's cause for optimism. Well, not exactly: Philippine life expectancy is just 71, it turns out, an age I have already surpassed.

Ok, let's discuss quality. "I'd seen those 'over the hill' birthday cards on store shelves, poking fun at crackling crones and forgetful geezers," one of those crackling crones wrote in a *Boston Globe* essay published in 2022. "We live in a youth-obsessed society... Age discrimination pervades every aspect of our culture..."

Indeed, it's true; here in the Philippines I've felt more respected, honored, cared for—even *admired*—than I ever did as a senior citizen in the United States. And yet, the yearning for more persists. More life, more love, more, well, more of *everything*.

Perhaps it's an impossible dream. Even jellyfish, one expert averred, are not immune to misfortune. "The fate of everything in the ocean... is to be eaten at some point," insists Monty Graham, a professor of integrative biology and director of the Florida Institute of Oceanography.

Pretty much, I guess, like the rest of us.

2.
PESTILENCE
June 2020 to October 2021

LONG DISTANCE LEARNING

My son, Isaac, has become a night owl.

Sometimes he does arithmetic while I try to sleep. Other nights he recites lessons in Filipino next to me in bed. And once I awoke to find him doing calisthenics in front of his laptop in the dark.

Welcome to online learning in the age of COVID with a twist; while Isaac is in California, his school is in the Philippines. So, as his fellow students start their lessons at 8 a.m., Isaac is almost ready for dinner. And when class resumes in the afternoon, he signs on in the dark of night.

All of which has wrought some major changes in our lives. Isaac and his mom, who helps prepare his lessons, have taken to going to bed late at night and getting up even later in the morning. Because the Philippines is 15 hours ahead of California, our weeks run from Sunday through Thursday. And so, I have become accustomed to hearing numbers, prayers, and Filipino sentences recited in my dreams.

That being said, online learning has, in some ways, exceeded our expectations. Back when it started, Isaac exhibited—shall we say—considerably less than full enthusiasm. Later, though, he warmed up to the idea, even reminding us to turn on the computer to prepare for class.

"Mommy, mommy," I've heard him say more than once, "did you forget it's time for *school*?" And these days he even seems to revel in donning his little Catholic schoolboy uniform—or at least its upper portions—to properly "meet" with his class.

Will any of this lead to real learning? On that score, I fear, the jury's still out. Part of the problem lies in the dearth of precedence for what's happening worldwide. In 2005, Hurricane Katrina destroyed over 100 schools in the southern United States, displacing thousands of students for months. A study conducted five years later revealed that over a third of them were academically behind their peers whose educations had remained uninterrupted. And many also had anxiety, depression and various other crisis-induced emotional woes.

Lisa Gibbs, a University of Melbourne researcher who studied the aftermath of Australian bushfires, found that "a changed academic pathway" in her subjects, "may have lifelong implications."

One obvious implication for my son—especially given his even *longer* long-distance learning—is lots more time for bike riding during these endless lazy days. To help effectuate that, we recently bought him a brand new 20-inch dirt bike with thick rubber cactus-ready tires. Ah, but nights are reserved for learning, with the verdict remaining unclear.

Will the absence of brick-and-mortar schools become part of the now-common characterization I loathe; the so-called "new normal?" Will the fact that Isaac can now "attend" school nearly 12,000 kilometers from where he sleeps make the significance of one's physical location obsolete?

And speaking of sleeping, will I ever again get my full share? That part of the equation, at least, bears a tentative solution; I'm thinking of buying wax earplugs.

PERMANENT DAMAGE

This morning we finally had the talk.

I'm sure you're familiar with it or, if you're a parent, probably engaged in it yourself. It's the one where you look your significant other squarely in the eye and ask, "What are we doing to our kid? Do you think the damage will be permanent?"

It's a conversation many parents have had since this damnable pandemic began. Upon leaving the Philippines, we expected US schools to reopen soon. And nearly half of them have. But not, unfortunately, those in our own rural Southern California school district, which recently announced that in-person learning won't resume until sometime this fall. As for the Philippines, God only knows when its schools will reopen. Sometimes I wonder if they *ever* will. That uncertain eventuality, however, is not something for which we are willing to hold our breaths.

And so every day around here is like every other day. My wife leaves for work early and gets home late. Our 18-month-old baby, Adira, born in the Philippines and now breathing American air for the very first time, spends part of each day with caregivers. And Isaac and I, well, we're mostly relegated to staying at home.

Which is fine with me, as I read several daily newspapers, stay abreast of current events, and devote much of my time to writing.

For Isaac, it's dicier; after spending a few hours feigning rapt interest in his online class, he usually passes the rest of the day glued hypnotically to one of his many available screens. Netflix, YouTube, Facebook, Xbox 1... you name it. If it's on a screen large or small, it keeps him completely transfixed for a very long haul. Blessed are the days — too few—on which he rides his bike outside with friends.

Fortunately, Isaac seems to be holding his own in what passes for education these days, though I suspect that has more to do with the help he's getting from his mom than with any overwhelming effort on his part. What worries me more, though, is the level of tension creeping into his relationship with both his mom and me.

"Isaac," I called to him this morning, same as *every* morning, "it's time for breakfast." When he hadn't appeared after 10 minutes, I tried again with a little more gusto. "Isaac!" I insisted a good deal louder, "come out and eat!" Finally, feeling my blood pressure rise, I yelled out his name while marching toward the closed bedroom door. Behind which I found him languishing under the covers in his underwear, watching the latest episode of *Super Mario Logan* on his mother's misplaced cell phone. "ISAAC!" I screamed at the top of my lungs, "come out right now!!!"

I suppose I could confiscate all those screens. But then, well, how in the world would he spend his time?

And so we had that special parental talk. "Gosh," I sighed with my wife nodding in ardent agreement, "if he acts like this now, what will he be like at 16?"

Neither of us is keen to find out. So we have vowed to keep calm. And speak to our son only in pleasant and reassuring whispers. As in, "Isaac, we love you; Now would you please put down that phone and come out to eat? Oh yes, and did we mention that we love you?"

If that doesn't work, we're cooked.

KIDS IN SPACE

The phone call startled me.

"David," my wife said from the medical lab 142 miles away where she works the night shift, "Grandpa is worried about Isaac."

She was referring, of course, to our son who, at that moment, was amusing himself in the living room where Ivy's father sat browsing on his cell phone while I watched TV in the bedroom.

"He says Isaac's doing this virtual reality thing," my wife went on, "and looks like he's gone insane. Please go out and check."

My first reaction was that if Grandpa had concerns regarding my son, he should knock on my door 20 feet away rather than bother my wife at work a two-and-a-half-hour drive away. My second reaction was that I better go check on my son.

What I found was not unlike what I'd seen before: Isaac gesticulating wildly into thin air, engaging in what appeared to be an imaginary conversation with someone only he could see. I should probably also mention that he was wearing a thick plastic wraparound mask completely covering his eyes and nose.

"Hey, son, how you doing in there?" I asked without receiving even a glimmer of response or recognition. "I hope everything's ok; your grandpa's kind of worried."

Welcome to the place where many of today's children live.

I should probably say, in my defense, that I'm not the one who initially opened its door to *this* child. No, that was my dear brother who, in a fit of generosity, swooped in one day to take his favorite nephew shopping. They returned with the brand-new Oculus Quest VR mask and controllers for which Isaac had been begging. And, well, our lives have never been the same.

For those unschooled in the vagaries of today's virtual reality universe, here's an elemental primer. It's not unlike, say, the gamers' cyberspace most of us have glimpsed online populated by dragons, demons, devils, and diehards. What *is* different, however, is that these monsters exist in real four-dimensional time projected in visual and audible stereo.

"Everything's good," Isaac assured me after I'd finally pried him away from his new mask. "Except that you just got me killed!"

Believe me, I've struggled with this. Is virtual reality, as his grandfather believes (informed, apparently, by a friend on Facebook) the road to dissonance, disaster, dysfunction, and despair? Or, as my pre-teen son insists, simply about frolicking, fanfare, flamboyance, and fun?

That very question formed the core of a recent conversation between me and an American friend. "Boy," he said, "I'm sure glad I don't have kids that age. You have to protect them, but you can't hide them from the world forever."

Even, I suppose, if that world exists in the cloud.

I was kind of stuck on the fence about it until Isaac said something that caught my attention. "Dad," he exclaimed, more excited than I'd seen him in years. "I've made a new friend!" Turns out the kid, who he met somewhere in virtual Lala land, actually lives in Wyoming. And now the two meet regularly in cyberspace to share their lives and adventures.

Would watching zombies on television, I asked myself, constitute a better use of his time? At least virtual reality is interactive. Not that different, I concluded, from playing cops-

and-robbers with your pals like I used to do as a youngster in the 1950s. And so, for now anyway, I've made peace with my son's virtual reality fixation within, of course, certain limits.

Ah, but now an additional threat lurks on the horizon sparking unprecedented and unexplored fears. Isaac claims not to have discovered girls yet, a major source of comfort for me and his mom. Our worst nightmare: that, when he finally does, his first girlfriend will be an AI Chatbot.

In which case, neither God nor Grandpa will be of much help.

STUCK BEHIND WALLS

It could be worse, of course.

I could be without Internet, TV and a view of the construction site next door. I could be somewhere without a restaurant downstairs that sends food up just for the dialing. And, let's face it, I could be in a place with gun-toting guards ordering pushups every morning.

Thankfully, I'm not. And yet I'm in prison, nonetheless, surrounded by four impenetrable walls. They will define my world for the next 10 days, or until powerful people wearing spacesuits deem me fit to rejoin society. Welcome to international travel in the age of COVID. More specifically, to the prolonged quarantine regimen facing foreigners entering—or, in my case, *re-entering*—a country called the Philippines.

Despite all evidence to the contrary, however, I'm really not complaining. For I brought this to myself by insisting on returning. And now am succored because, well, I finally got my wish. Please allow me a small digression to tell you how it happened.

As I explained earlier, Southern California recently ensnared me. What began as a few-months sojourn, however, stretched into a much-longer time. And so I've been going with the flow, completing tasks that needed doing while enjoying the proximity of long-lost relatives and friends in America. But recently, it became apparent that my prolonged absence could jeopardize the permanent-resident status I enjoy in the

Philippines. And so I made plans to return, despite having to leave the family behind. The reason for departing solo: to allow young Isaac the potential and much-anticipated benefits of in-class learning after way too long of what has passed for "learning" in front of a screen.

But saying goodbye to my beautiful wife and children proved harder than I'd ever imagined. Driving away after bidding the kids farewell, both Ivy and I cried. And parting from her at the airport rendered a repeat of that ungainly spectacle.

Ah, but anxiety soon replaced grief. Had I remembered to bring the long list of required documents? If I forgot something, would it delay my trip? It wasn't confidence-inspiring to hear that a family of friends attempting the same journey a few days earlier had been denied boarding passes because they couldn't produce the birth certificate of their Filipino/American son. Nor was I buoyed to read that Philippine President Rodrigo Duterte was once again considering completely shutting the country down.

So I focused on doing what had to be done. Five days prior to departure, I registered on a government website to be issued the requisite barcode. I also downloaded the indicated tracing app to my phone, filled out several questionnaires, and carefully prepared a folder full of documents. Finally, I booked 10 nights at a government-certified hotel in Cebu for the required, strictly enforced quarantine.

The flight was as uneventful as it was long. Two hours prior to landing, the crew gave each passenger more papers to fill out. And then we were in the terminal at Mactan-Cebu International Airport waiting in long lines for briefings, documents and temperature checks. All to be followed by swab testing of our noses and throats, baggage retrieval, and, finally, rides to our respective hotels.

So here I am, confined behind four walls. The room isn't bad; it's got a bed, closet, minibar, soaking-wet bathroom and the aforementioned window looking out on that abandoned building site. A nice young woman delivers breakfast each morning at my door; the rest I have to order by phone. There's a TV, though the volume's too low and my favorite channels are missing. And, while tempted to loll the time away in pajamas, I try daily to put on some clothes.

On the seventh day, I'm told, one of those spacesuit-clad strangers will reemerge for another swabbing. Then, barring any unfortunate swab-related surprises, three days after that I will be free to continue to my Philippine home. Where, once again, I'll need to quarantine for four more days. Ah, but this time, thank God, I will be in my own house. Which, the last time I checked, had considerably more space between its four walls.

NO PLACE LIKE HOME

The moment was sweet.

Hunkered down in my home office in Mindanao, I heard a commotion downstairs and decided to investigate. There, without apology or explanation, stood a gaggle of relatives and friends, each smiling broadly.

"Welcome home, David," someone said, pointing to a cake bearing my name. Everyone applauded. And instantly, I knew I was in just the right place. After a 15-hour flight, two swab tests, 10 days of confinement in a small hotel room and a nine-hour ferry ride, I was finally back in the beautiful house my wife and I built overlooking the placid waters of Surigao Strait.

"I can't tell you how glad I am to be here," I stammered. And then came the fabulous feast.

It is moments like these that remind me anew of why I love the Philippines. Hands down, it's the warmth of the culture and its practitioners, and their desire to acknowledge individually everyone's importance as part of the whole. In short, it is a country celebratory to its core.

It's also a place, especially lately, in the clutches of considerable pain.

That fact hit me as soon as I got off the plane into what amounted to a fear hurricane. To be sure, people everywhere are concerned about COVID-19, particularly its recently emerged variant dubbed Delta. Health officials in the US, in fact, had nearly declared victory before this fresh problem emerged. Los Angeles County, which had already lifted a much-maligned mask mandate, reimposed it. And, as usual, the public's response ranged from reverence to rancor.

Lockdowns and mandates in the Philippines are significantly stricter. Last week, Interior Secretary Eduardo Año warned residents of Metro Manila to stay home or risk arrest.

"We will be strict in this," he said. "We need to be. If you won't comply and insist on going outside, of course, we will arrest you."

The initial response was the ironic "super spreader" spectacle of thousands of residents literally clamoring over each other to get vaccinated before the lockdown began. And, true to Año's promise, by week's end police had apprehended at least 20,600 suspects in Manila and neighboring provinces for offenses including curfew violation, failing to wear, or improperly wearing masks and face shields, disregarding social distancing protocols, and engaging in "mass" gatherings. Penalties included fines, community service and charges that could lead to imprisonment.

Several provinces in Luzon, meanwhile, have literally posted guards at their gates to maintain stringent border control. Only those from unaffected areas are allowed entry, and only with negative COVID tests.

Police in Bugo, a *barangay* of Cagayan de Oro, even arrested an evangelical Christian pastor for conducting prayer meetings in his home. "Only virtual religious gatherings are allowed..." Police Major Evan Viñas said.

Despite the higher likelihood of death among Americans, the average Filipino's reaction has been relatively subdued. Though both countries show COVID fatality rates of about 1.7%, according to numbers compiled by the Johns Hopkins University School of Medicine, the deaths per 100,000 population are many times greater in the US.

So why are so many Filipinos, particularly in rural areas, embracing these strict measures without hesitation? Part of the answer lies in an Asian culture emphasizing obedience and personal sacrifice for the greater good. And, too, the relative devastation of the Philippine economy has given many of its citizens more immediate concerns.

So instead of lobbying for lighter lockdowns, Filipinos are seeking other kinds of aid. “We didn’t eat today,” texted one journalist friend, whose place of work has been indefinitely closed. “We have no money, and we have no food. We pray to God that you can help.”

Though acquainted on Facebook, we have never actually met. Yet she felt desperate enough to put her pride aside and ask for help. And she’s not alone; hardly a week goes by that I don’t get at least one such request.

Soon, I expect to emerge from my mandatory week-long home quarantine. I have already received the city’s coveted Health Pass required for entry into public places. And so, it seems, I shall finally be back in the world. Wearing a tight-fitting mask. Oh yes, and a properly worn face shield.

What can I say, it ain’t California.

BACK ON TRACK

His excitement was palpable.

"Daddy," Isaac announced from the dimly lit screen of my cell phone, "I made a new friend!"

It had been a long time since I'd seen my son so animated. But this was his first day of school in Southern California, not online but in a physical classroom. And as I watched his fluttering image from the Philippines, my dear little son seemed reawakened before my eyes.

God, how I longed to hug him. Lord, how I missed his baby sister and mom standing there beside him. Being away from them was a sacrifice, no doubt. But it was one I was willing to make for the benefit of my son.

"Good for you, Isaac," I said, choking down the growing lump in my throat. "I'm glad your first day went well."

Then we hung up, and I was alone.

It's been nearly a year since President Duterte's declaration that Philippine classrooms would remain closed until something convinced him they were safe to reopen. Which, as I've said, eventually imposed our painful choice of returning to California where, after nine months of what everyone euphemistically called online "education", the schools finally succumbed to the loud public clamor to reopen their doors. Not too long after my solo return to the Philippines to take care of such pressing matters as renewing my visa and checking on our house.

But what's amazed me most in the wake of my return is the complete lack of rancor regarding this country's still-shuttered schools. Why isn't anyone complaining?

Believe me, it isn't because of unusually high COVID numbers. Many places that have recommenced normal education have infection rates equaling or exceeding those of the Philippines. In fact, this is one of only five countries worldwide that has not resumed in-person teaching, the others being Bangladesh, Kuwait, Saudi Arabia, and Venezuela.

Science is barely involved. Children, since the beginning of the pandemic, have enjoyed significantly lower infection rates than adults. And those who do get sick generally experience only mild symptoms, seldom requiring hospitalization and rarely resulting in death. A recent study by the US Centers for Disease Control and Prevention found that in Los Angeles County, where I grew up, the case rates among children attending school from September 2020 through March 2021, were, in fact, dramatically *lower* than those of children overall.

And yet the impact on youngsters kept out of school is significant and pronounced. "The associated consequences of school closure—learning loss, mental distress, missed vaccinations, and heightened risk of dropout, child labor, and child marriage—will be felt by many children," Oyunsaikhan Dendevnorov, the Philippines' representative to the United Nations Children's Fund, said in a recent statement by that agency calling for the schools to reopen.

Citing various studies, an accompanying report asserts that a young person's positive experiences in elementary school are a predictor of future social, emotional, and educational outcomes. The report concludes that those who fall behind in school remain behind for the rest of their time there, and eventually that gap grows.

So why aren't more Filipinos raising their voices in protest? In my home state of California, the public outcry against prolonged school closures, among other issues, grew adamant enough to force the governor into an upcoming recall election that could remove him from office. And yet here in the Philippines, the relative silence is hurting my ears.

And so I wait. And wonder. And hope for a day when my family can reunite beyond Christmas.

Oh, yes, and enjoy that daily long-distance video chat with my highly excited son. “I had a fantastic day,” he assured me last night. “Being back at school just makes me so happy!”

ZOOM WEDDING

The bride looked radiant in her glowing white gown.

Directly behind her sat Mom and Dad; she beaming proudly holding a flower while he stared painfully wearing a stiffly ironed barong. Front-and-center, clutching something close to her bosom where one might expect a rose, Maryneil Guarte, the soon-to-be new wife, held tightly onto... wait... a cell phone?

Say hello to what may soon become the "new normal"– courtship and marriage, courtesy of Zoom.

This wasn't exactly the wedding she'd planned. Guarte, 24, met her American now-husband, 23-year-old Nyuim White, last year the same way many transnational couples meet these days; on an internet dating site called Filipino Cupid. "He was just so kind," she recalls. "He really understands me."

Like most Fil Am couples, they chatted, wrote, and zoomed until they fell in love. Unlike most until recently, however, their romance got rudely interrupted by the humorless COVID pandemic.

It all happened so quickly they hardly knew what hit them. Guarte invited White, a roofer from Murietta, Georgia, to attend a family reunion in her hometown of Cantilan, Surigao del Sur. The potential husband—a fan of the popular TV series "90 Day Fiancé"—quickly bought a ticket. Then the pandemic hit, the Philippines closed its borders and boom!, the rest you can probably imagine.

Though they had yet to meet in person, White proposed to her late last year. At first Guarte turned him down, wishing to avoid what she calls a "Tik Tok wedding." But after months of ongoing lockdowns, her heart underwent a change.

There's only one jurisdiction in America—and perhaps the entire world—that performs legal marriages online and that's Utah County, Utah. The rules are simple; the bride and groom can be anywhere, either together or apart, as long as the officiating officer has both feet firmly planted in the aforementioned county.

And so it came to pass on a recent afternoon (or wee-early morning depending on your geographic perspective) that Maryneil and Nyuim became Mr. and Mrs. White as dozens of eyeballs watched from half as many screens. It was 1 p.m. in Utah, 3 p.m. in Georgia, and 3 a.m. in Cantilan.

"It felt kind of weird," Maryneil now admits. "You're talking, but you can't hear because there are lots of people in the background. Our connection was terrible, but I was too scared to ask them to repeat. It was hilarious."

Yet love always finds a way, and so they got the deed done. Nyuim is planning his first-ever visit to the Philippines in December. "I can't hug him at the airport because he needs to be quarantined for 10 days in a hotel," Maryneil laments. "But I will try to wave."

Eventually, she says, she hopes to emigrate to America where the couple will buy a house and car.

But there was one last burning question just begging for an answer. What, exactly, I wondered, had they done upon hearing those fateful closing words: "you now may kiss the bride"?

Oh, that's easy, Maryneil replied, "we threw flying kisses."

OUCH!

He squealed like a pig being slaughtered.

But this was no pig. It was my eight-year-old nephew. And the slaughter wasn't a hog being gutted for fiesta.

No, this was a somewhat less lethal procedure though, judging from his screams, perhaps just as traumatic. The slicing away of an anatomical sliver to which he was, well...quite *attached.* The snipping of his foreskin, that seemingly useless bit of flesh sheathing the penis with which all boys are born but, in the Philippines, seldom keep for long.

In normal times, those bothersome pinkish globs are clipped en mass during summer clinics held at health centers and school gymnasiums nationwide. But with tiny killer microbes lurking about, these times are hardly normal. And so it came to pass that a friendly local nurse made a house call to perform the deed on our dining room table.

I should probably mention here that I am certainly no stranger to the rite of circumcision. In fact, I have survived the procedure myself, as have my sons. But here's the thing; none of us remembers the shearing of our private parts because it happened when we were just days old. In the Philippines, it's different. Boys aren't even considered eligible for pruning until age six and remain eligible until, well...the thing gets done.

As strange as it may seem, this wasn't even the first time I'd witnessed older boys getting carved. That happened 30 years ago when, as a reporter for the *Los Angeles Times*, I covered an event that—by American standards anyway—seemed quite bizarre; the ritualistic cutting of newly arrived Jewish immigrants at a hospital in California.

See, in Judaism, circumcision is viewed as a religious rite marking a special "covenant" with God. Traditionally performed by a rabbi at home when the baby is eight days old, the gala event involves friends and family who recite lots of blessings and say lots of prayers. After which, of course, they eat lots of food and drink lots of wine.

These particular immigrants, however, had come from the former Soviet Union, where such religious rituals were strictly forbidden. So they were more than happy to have their young sons—aged two to 12—submit to the rabbi's knife under the watchful eye of a surgeon. My most vivid memory of that day is the long line of crumpled foreskins on the table at its end.

My own youngest son, also born in the United States, had the opposite problem; instead of being too old, he was almost too young. We knew that because the doctor suggested waiting a month until his you-know-what got a little bit bigger. We agreed, but then another doctor, claiming to be an expert on the matter, insisted on immediate action.

And so we took it, as did he.

I'll never forget the moment they brought our new baby out of the operating room. Where his penis had been now lay a bloody crevice. "Oh my God," I screamed, "they've cut it off!" Fortunately, time proved me wrong; eventually that tiny, traumatized member once again peaked timidly out from its raggedy little foxhole and, eventually, became even bolder.

But now it was his Filipino cousin's turn, and not a moment too soon. Twice he ran out the front door, only to be retrieved blocks away by his sprinting older brother. And then, with his mother holding him down and a gaggle of grinning relatives taking pictures, the poor boy screamed as the nurse wielded scissors where we'd served breakfast just before.

"It's easier when they're younger," she later admitted, adding that her oldest patient had been 17.

And that's how I passed the morning of my last day under general community quarantine. Everything's back to normal now except for just one thing; an unsmiling little boy is limping around in pain.

SCAMMING FOR CAUSE

It happens at least once a week.

I get a message on Facebook from someone I don't know. "Hi," the inquiring stranger always begins, "how are you?"

I am friendly by nature. And, perhaps more-to-the-point, I have an intuitive curiosity honed by years professionally sticking my nose into other people's business.

"Hello there," I usually respond. "I'm fine. How are *you*?"

And so the dialog begins.

Before answering my question, the new text mate, usually a young woman, engages in some small talk. Then, invariably, "not so good," she replies. "My (and here you can fill in the blanks) *mother, brother, sister, cousin* is sick," or "my rice pail is empty," or "I haven't worked in months."

All of which is probably true. Or maybe not.

Last week I got a gut-wrencher: "My little boy died and I can't afford the funeral."

As a foreigner in the Philippines, especially one with white skin, I've grown accustomed to this kind of attention. In the early days, it came mostly in the form of urban cab drivers upping their fares, or children following me in the streets with hands outstretched. At first I gave them coins. Then realized that I was attracting enough kids to form my own marching band.

More recently, I learned a similar lesson on Facebook, where the plaintive cries for help have increased exponentially in the wake of the pandemic. Touched by their tragic tales, I sent cash to more than a few. Which almost always resulted in a never-ending series of increasingly dreadful requests. And so I made the reluctant decision to help only relatives and friends.

That's when I heard from the young woman I'll call Shirley. "Hi," she messaged, "how are you?" And so, as usual, our dialogue began. Shirley shared that she was a single mother with a young son who'd lost her job because of the pandemic. Could I find it in my heart to help her buy food?

As tempting as it was, I stuck to my newfound resolve. "I'm so sorry," I said, explaining my recent decision.

"I understand," she replied. "Whatever happens, I like you. Always stay safe and take care of your family."

The next day she hit me with this: "I don't have rice, no work because of the lockdown, and my son is sick, Jesus Christ!" Sending a string of sobbing emojis, she continued her plea. "I know we're not relatives, but open your heart. Please, from God, I wish you can give."

I felt myself wavering.

The next day she told me her son was in the hospital with asthma, and the day after that she said he had died. Oh my God, I thought, am I responsible for the death of this child? Now please, she pleaded, could you just help pay for the funeral?

By then, however, I'd noticed some discrepancies. Shirley's Facebook profile omitted any mention of a son. The pictures she'd sent, ostensibly from the hospital, never showed them together in a frame. And somehow her timing seemed suspiciously convenient.

Fortunately, there was an easy way to discover the truth. The funeral parlor she'd mentioned was not far away. And as I drove towards it, God forgive me, I almost hoped he'd be there. If so, I decided, I would offer my condolences and foot the whole bill.

But he wasn't there, only three dead adults. And the manager had no memory of having recently hosted a child. When I gently broke the news to Shirley, she reacted with defiance. "I don't have to explain," she snapped. "I know you're happy now."

Then she blocked me from all further contact.

She's wrong about me being happy. I'm not happy that so many Filipinos feel desperate enough to lie about their circumstances. Not happy that I usually have to say no. And certainly not happy to see an otherwise proud culture humbled by a microbe.

Here's my prayer for Shirley and others like her; that those microbes fade to fiction so their children can rise to real.

THE HOUSE ON THE HILL

He could sometimes be disagreeable.

A man with strong opinions, he seldom held them back. And whatever inner filters most of us download to preempt the reactions of others, well, Les had somehow neglected to install.

And yet he was a true original, a man extremely hard to forget. He was a builder and a dreamer whose dreams infected others. Last week, he died in his sleep, leaving some of those dreams unfulfilled. So this week I am contemplating a world without Les.

Like me, he was an American expat married to a Filipina. I must have met him around 2008, probably at one of the many parties he used to host for Americans and their Filipino wives living in Southern California. Les was already a veteran of that burgeoning culture, having married lovely Ruthie four years earlier. And so, being a newbie, I relied upon his guidance.

In one of our first conversations, he mentioned the house on the hill. It didn't yet exist, Les said, except in his mind. He would build it on a hilltop lot he and his wife owned in Cebu, offering a panoramic view of the city. It would feature plenty of windows, a swimming pool, and, oh yes, "his" and "her" bathrooms because Les didn't like to share. Besides being a Vietnam veteran, he had worked in construction, which made his dream easy to embrace.

As time passed, Les and I became friends. Sometimes we'd meet for drinks with other American husbands married to Filipinas to swap stories about our wives and their families. Or entertain each other with exaggerated tales of our heroic exploits abroad. My favorite discussions, though, always centered on the details he'd add to those storied building plans like sprinkling sugar on top of a cake.

Over the years, the parties became less frequent as people bought houses and began having kids. Ivy and I concocted our own dream of building a house in the Philippines. But Les and Ruthie were among the first to actually migrate across the Pacific.

Once, during a visit to Cebu, he showed me the lot he had described. It was everything he'd said it was and more; a perch that would bless any man with the fortitude to tame it. But people change and so do their dreams. Eventually, Les and Ruthie bought a home in the city, added a townhouse for extra income, and embarked on the newer dream of building a Mexican restaurant overlooking Cebu.

"Do you have any experience running restaurants?" someone asked him. No worries, Les allegedly responded, he would learn to make tortillas on YouTube. You gotta love a guy like that—if one could live on dreams alone, Les would have lived forever.

Alas, one can't. And so last week, just shy of his 78th birthday, a massive heart attack whisked him away. Ruthie says her husband had a history of heart problems resulting in the insertion of a coronary stent while still in America. After moving to Cebu, she says, he took lots of meds and made biannual pilgrimages to see a VA specialist in Manila. The COVID pandemic ended that. And so Les died, yet another victim of this damnable international scourge.

When I think of him now, all that fades away. What I see is a man whose dreams sustained him until the end. A man whose visions were bigger than he was. And, yes, a man gazing out the window of that mythic house on the hill.

DANCING IN THE STREETS

It happened again.

People wearing ornate, many-colored costumes swirled in the streets to the cadence of drummers in trucks. Expressions of joy, even ecstasy, lit up their youthful faces. And, as always, the air above them seemed tinged with the bright yellow hue of life celebrating itself.

I had seen it all before, of course, and written about it frequently. But there were two big differences at this year's *Banok-Banok* street-dancing fiesta in Surigao City. First, it revived an annual tradition that COVID had felled for two years. And, finally, for the first time, I imagined my little girl's face among the whirling dancers in the streets.

As I've explained before, the event highlights the city's annual fiesta designed to celebrate the lives and legends of the indigenous *Mamanwa* tribe. They were the region's first inhabitants, long before the Spanish conquistadors bearing swords arrived with their padres bearing crosses. But the event also pays tribute to the city's patron saint, St. Nicholas de Tolentino, an Italian mystic often invoked on behalf of the suffering souls in purgatory. Which, I suppose, made him the perfect protector during those long COVID lockdowns.

But here's the point: anyone willing to rise early enough to navigate fiesta traffic gets to gaze upon the remarkable sight of bright-eyed Filipinos dressed in native garb swooning over statuettes of a Catholic saint. It's a wonderful confluence of religion and culture representing what the Philippines has become; a young country combining the best of a rich history with a percolating present pregnant with potential.

Back in 2019, watching the parade evoked the feeling that, as I've said many times, I sometimes get while watching a beautiful sunset or admiring a placid blue sea. Certain pieces of music have the same effect, as do my favorite works of art, literary passages and even cinematic scenes.

That was about the time I first learned my wife was expecting another child. We visited an obstetrician's office in Cebu, where we stared at a small screen as the grainy image from an ultrasound slowly took shape. There, unmistakably, lay a tiny arm stretched out above our baby's head. Then, as we both held our breaths, the air suddenly pulsated with the sound of a tiny heartbeat. And that's when knew God was present. Just as I did last week when the beat of my heart matched the pulse of those drums.

Adira is two now and already loves to dance. Her favorite song is "Let it Go," the theme from Disney's animated movie, *Frozen*. "Let it go, let it go, I am one with the wind and sky," Elsa sings, as Adira hums along, mouthing the words while throwing her arms open and stomping to the beat. "Let it go, let it go, you'll never see me cry."

I dream of the day when my beloved little girl dances in the streets of Surigao. I surely hope to be watching.

3.
DELUGE
December 2021 to November 2022

SEVERELY DAMAGED

We finally got the bad news at 1:45 in the morning.

It hadn't been even two weeks since I'd returned from the Philippines after renewing my visa and taking stock of the dream house we'd built by the sea. Only to learn of the severe damage caused by a Category Five typhoon's ruthless attacked from the sky.

"Surigao City around 75% damaged, but locals recovering," a good friend reported on Facebook after driving several miles out of town to find an internet signal. "More for Siargao and Dinagat. Estimate is four to six months to restore power in Surigao."

We had been bracing for bad news, but hoping it would be better. For several days we'd been scouring Facebook, increasingly shocked at the burgeoning slash of videos showing the utter devastation. A few hours before that post, another one had grabbed our attention. In it, a young man is documenting the damage to Punta Bilar, our home barangay, when suddenly a voice in the background comments, "Did you see that big house on the hill; it's missing half its roof!"

Ivy and I looked at each other, our eyes widening with horror. "Hon," she quietly intoned. "That sounds like *our* house."

In fact, it was the first bit of news we'd received since the moment, five days earlier, that we'd lost contact with Ivy's sister who shares that big house on the hill. Eva had just shown us, in a live video feed, the swaying trees and thundering raindrops outside our beloved home's windows. Suddenly, the image reverted to her face. "Oh no," she said, "water's pouring in through the broken windows upstairs!" Then the feed went dead, leaving us to the darkness of our grim imaginations.

After enduring long days and nights of silence, we finally heard from her last night. She and the family are shaken but fine, she said, from somewhere en route to a cousin's house three hours down the coast in Butuan. Then she sent us pictures of what the house looks like now, confirming our worst fears. The roof, windows, ceilings, floors, even the white gazebo, recently blessed by a priest, are all gone.

The inside of the upper story looks like a disaster area, strewn with broken glass and debris. Furniture, art, air conditioning, computers, books, photos, mementos, and awards, all blown away.

But amidst the chaos, miraculously, gleams a silver lining: the basic structure seems to have held. To the extent, Eva tells us, that in the depths of this ferocious storm at least five families whose houses had blown away found shelter for several days in the basement of ours.

Somehow that affords a level of comfort, even in the depths of despair.

Fortunately, our family and friends are all safe. Yet the number of known casualties keeps rising; as of this week, *NBC* reports, nearly 400 have died overall, though only a handful in our general area. We pray those numbers don't increase.

The survivors, many without roofs over their heads, are facing critical shortages of food and water, as well as the inability to communicate with anyone outside. Fortunately, the Philippine Red Cross has stepped in, delivering five tons of food every day. And our friends' generous offers of support have been heartening.

Early in our ancient plans to make Surigao our home, every sign stood in our favor and every traffic light glowed green. When we first bought the land upon which our house now stands, I'd felt that God had smiled on our little union of culture, nation and faith here on this hilltop in Punta Bilar. Then came COVID, forcing a temporary retreat to California, and now this, further delaying my family's return and my re-return.

So what's the main takeaway from all this tragedy and disaster? For me, it's simply this: that life stands poised on a dime. That, no matter how happy and stable one's existence may seem, everything can change in an instant. It also confirms my long-held suspicion that God has a wicked sense of humor.

We, of course, will try to rebuild. In a few months, after the dust has settled and the power's restored, I shall travel to Surigao once more to survey the damage and assess where we stand. For now, though, our only options are to pray, encourage, and assist where we can.

SWEPT AWAY

It was only a typewriter.

An antique machine upon which, many years ago, I began to write. Now it sat idly on a shelf, reminding me of my sparse beginnings.

There were other mementos in that home office overlooking Surigao Strait: photographs of me in my early days as a reporter riding elephants and chasing hot air balloons; the tangle of press credentials once dangling at my chest; and an array of trophies, commendations and ribbons representing the high points of a career much enjoyed. One was a prized glass plaque certifying participation in the Pulitzer-winning coverage of the Los Angeles riots in 1992. Others included literary awards for my 2015 memoir, *Nazis & Nudists*, and a Golden Mike presented for excellence in radio broadcasting.

There was also a compilation of books autographed by their authors—many of them my friends—as well as the mosaic of a magazine piece recounting the wooing of my Filipino wife and, perhaps my favorite, a pair of golden mouse ears earned while covering Disneyland's 50th anniversary in 2005.

All of it is gone now, swept away by Typhoon Odette. And so I am left to contemplate life without those bolstering tokens of my past.

In truth, no one ever noticed them but me. Yet in that gaze lay a lifetime of memories. The people I worked with and the stories I covered. The big ones that got away and the smaller ones I lassoed. None of them made me rich or famous. But, in the evening of my life, they have helped succor my continued existence.

What will do that now that all of it has disappeared?

It may seem like a frivolous question to those still young. But others of a certain age will doubtless understand the tendency to hang onto the past with an earnestness commensurate to its volume. It's as if those relics constitute proof that you existed. As if, without them, somehow you were never here at all.

Ah, but maybe there's a hidden message in the reckless wreckage of those ancient tokens. Perhaps this catastrophic cleansing portends the dawn of a new reckoning and sense of self. In fact, that's what I've been trying to grasp in the wake of this dastardly disturbance. Instead of thinking of *then*, I'm attempting to consider the *now*. Instead of mourning the past, I am endeavoring to embrace the future. And rather than cry over what's been lost, I am striving to discern what's been gained.

Thankfully, I'm getting glimpses of just what that is. I see it in the efforts of those who've lost much to help those who've lost more. In the prayers of people simply happy to be alive. And, finally, I see it in the warm embrace of my wonderful wife and the sweet smiles of my beautiful children.

Perhaps there's no better time than now to grasp new horizons by drawing close those we hold dear. And so, to you who are suffering and you who are not, I wish all a happy New Year.

GONE WITH THE WIND

There was something comforting about living across the street from a monument to history.

On Tuesday mornings, we'd hear the bright strains of reverie as the flags of four nations awoke to a new week. And every Sunday evening, the sad bugle tones of taps wafted through the air as those flags got lowered to the ground.

Sometimes I'd saunter over to gaze at the relics housed in the new museum. The display included maps, ship models, and pieces of World War II Japanese naval uniforms. There was also an old portrait of David Mattiske, a former Australian sailor and one of the last survivors of the historic event the museum recounted. He died earlier this year at 96. Then Typhoon Odette swept away all those relics, museum roof, and walls.

"Very little was saved," says Jake Miranda, our former divemaster and history buff whose efforts culminated in the Battle of Surigao Strait Memorial and Museum, arguably Surigao City's most popular attraction. Many of the lost relics, in fact, came from Miranda's personal collection.

The memorial was still just a dream back in 2013 when we bought the lot at Punta Bilar where he once brought us ashore near the place where our house now stands. The spot overlooks Surigao Strait, the historic gateway to Mindanao through which Magellan's ships passed in 1521. Over 420 years later, in 1944, another historic event transpired there; the Battle of Surigao Strait, which changed the course of World War II in the Pacific, paving the way for the Allied liberation of the Philippines from Imperial Japan. That fight was the largest—and probably last—major naval battle in human history.

After a year of construction, officials inaugurated the new memorial and museum in 2019 just in time for that year's commemoration of the battle on Oct. 25th. It was a grand affair, attended by Mattiske himself as well as dignitaries from all four nations that had taken part in the conflagration: Japan, Philippines, Australia and the US. It was also the last time the site hosted the event before COVID. The following year saw the commemoration shift online, and the subsequent year witnessed a significant downsizing.

Then that furious Category Five typhoon hit, opening the museum like a can opener and destroying most of its contents. The eternal flame once gracing the memorial's center has also disappeared, as have the trees and plants that gave it peaceful succor. Still visible, however, are the eternal words of Mattiske engraved in a concrete wall: "Let us pray that we never have another world war."

For the time being, the memorial remains closed to the multitude of visitors that began arriving almost from the moment it first opened. And the sounds of the weekly flag-raising ceremonies no longer pervade the silence of our broken house.

Miranda hopes to restore at least some of what the storm took away. The city has vowed to make repairs, though obviously that cruel and destructive storm has overburdened Surigao's plate. Miranda says he's also talking to a private cement company about possibly adopting and repairing the site. And many of Mattiske's Australian friends are offering to help in the deceased mariner's honor.

All of which reminds me of my first reaction to the raising of those flags just three years ago. I was struck by how different the four national anthems sounded. Australia's was young, optimistic, and proud; America's historic, grateful and proud; and the Philippines' majestic, optimistic and, yes, proud. Only Japan's national anthem sounded like a funeral dirge.

I pray it won't be the last one we hear

THANKS VERY BIG

The video is hard to watch without getting emotional.

In it, dozens of neighbors gather at the Siargao Island home of my in-laws, one of the few left standing in the wake of the super typhoon. As a relative unloads bags of rice from a parked mini cab, the crowd can barely contain its growing excitement.

"*Salamat karadjao*!" several exclaim, expressing gratitude in their native tongue. Then, after hoisting a bag onto her sagging shoulder, a middle-aged woman tries it in English. "Thanks very big!" she says, grinning broadly before disappearing into the crowd. And that's when the tickle in my throat becomes a lump that threatens to explode.

Friends and relatives here in America sowed the seeds of that lump. It began with our description on Facebook of the climatic calamity in the Philippines. Without our even asking, people immediately started contributing what they could. The bottom line: nearly 165,000 pesos—more than $3200—collected in just a few days. And so some residents of my wife's birthplace will have plenty to eat, at least for a while.

That wasn't the only help to pour in. An online group composed of Ivy and several others from that same provincial neighborhood—a previously charming little barangay called Caridad—raised enough to buy several solar panels, solar-powered streetlamps, and a diesel generator for their hometown. Thus at least some residents will have access to electricity during the long months likely to pass before government workers can repair thousands of downed and disabled power lines.

Many other friends on Siargao Island and in Surigao City—most of them struggling themselves—organized fundraisers, as did people from various locations worldwide. And, of course, there was help from government entities, both in the Philippines and abroad, as well as several international nonprofits.

All of which has helped renew my faith in the basic goodness of humankind.

That faith also seems to be spreading in Surigao City where the typhoon destroyed nearly 24,000 homes and damaged another 19,500, including our own. "The survivors' ability to take misfortune lightly and see the brighter side of things indicates a resilient attitude that bodes well for their eventual recovery," the *Philippine Daily Inquirer* reported in a Jan.2, 2022 story headlined "Surigao folks see hope in New Year amid typhoon ruins."

And yet moments of despair remain. On New Year's Day, I viewed a videotaped greeting from my sister-in-law bearing pictures of our once-sterling living room overlooking Surigao Strait. It's still beautiful and, thank God, mostly intact. But above her smiling face gaped a giant hole dangling torn electrical wiring from the ceiling. And a corner once graced by my favorite hand-carved wooden sculpture now offers only a wide-open space.

"Jeez," I muttered to my dear and patient wife, "I kind of forgot about all the damage." Tomorrow, the civil engineer who helped build our house will assess its condition, beginning with the tattered roof and shattered windows. The original art and family heirlooms blown away or destroyed inside, of course, we can never recover or replace.

Through it all, though, I am succored by the knowledge that it could have been oh so much worse. Just this morning, a grim television news story jerked me out of a forgetful and pleasant sleep. A wildfire in Colorado had destroyed nearly 1,000 homes and 6,000 acres.

"Unfortunately for myself and the neighbors," a distraught father told Channel Nine, "all the houses on [our street] are burned down to cinder blocks in the basement. We are a little devastated. I hope that nobody has been killed... because lives are more important than physical structures that we can replace."

To which I offer a heartfelt amen.

SLAUGHTERED PLANS

I'm working in my pajamas today.

I had expected to spend the week touring castles in the United Kingdom rather than writing columns in California. The manner in which those plans devolved from castles to casuals, however, perfectly illustrates how our society is descending from relative order to dystopian chaos.

Our original plan was not complicated. After spending way too long banished from domestic bliss in the Philippines due, first, to a pitiless pandemic and then to a tyrannical typhoon, we had finally arranged for a rollicking return. But with my wife's 40th birthday approaching, she also wanted to do something special. So we followed a friend's advice and bought discounted "promo" tickets from an outfit called Wind Travel Pattaya.

Working with Filipino agents in London and Thailand, we booked the perfect diversion: a flight from Los Angeles to the UK, followed two weeks later by another one from London to Manila. I began sensing something was amiss, however, several weeks later when no confirmation or itinerary had arrived.

Not to worry, our friend explained, Virgin Atlantic would issue us tickets 10 days prior to departure. When that didn't happen, the agent alleged that the airline was super busy and would certify us 24 hours before takeoff. That soon became 15, then eight. And that's when I called the airline directly, only to learn that the flight we thought we were on no longer existed and we had yet to be booked on another.

"We've never had a customer unable to fly," the person we now laughingly referred to as our "travel agent" confidently assured us. Though our boarding may be delayed, he said, "just go to the airport to wait for the release of your tickets."

And that's when I ran out of patience. I'm sorry, I told him, but there was no way I'd be going to the airport ticketless with a wife, two young children, and more than 10 heavy parcels in tow. Not to mention the fact that our California residence was located nearly three hours from the airport by car.

To be honest, we never learned whether the ticketing delay had resulted from a scam or, more likely, a radical case of incompetence. Whichever the case, our decision to stay where we were got confirmed almost immediately by some disturbing news from Great Britain. London's Heathrow Airport, the BBC reported, was overwhelmed and in chaos with dozens of flights canceled and airport personnel threatening to strike.

The situation was "awful," one passenger lamented. "There were hundreds of people there, some sleeping on the floor." Not to be outdone, American media immediately chimed in with stories of local airports deluged with passengers and flight cancelations in anticipation of the July 4th holiday weekend.

So here we sit in Joshua Tree, California, literally living out of suitcases in our own home. "Wow," a friend sighed when I told him of our plight. "This is not the country we grew up in—it's becoming an underdeveloped nation."

Bottom line: we've decided to skip England altogether and fly directly to the Philippines. "Sorry, not today," our new travel agent told us this morning.

Ah, but we still have great hopes for tomorrow.

TIME TRAVEL

It's as if our return to the Philippines was a step back in time.

Outside our storied window lies a pile of decaying debris. The veranda has no roof and some of our doors are still missing. And, to add insult to injury, we are once again reduced to living out of suitcases downstairs rather than reveling in the spacious bedroom above.

The last time that happened was in 2018, when we first moved into our seaside house, then still under construction. This time it's because, a full seven months after Super Typhoon Odette (also known as Typhoon Rai), the house hasn't yet recovered from nearly getting blown away.

I should have sensed trouble in the foreboding obstacles we encountered en route to our long-anticipated return. Last week I wrote about how we had to scrap a planned trip to Europe because the tickets we thought we'd bought were for a flight that didn't exist. Eventually, we scored a refund and booked another flight five days later directly to Cebu. Well, not exactly; it included a two-hour layover in Taipei, Taiwan. Which is why, upon arriving at Los Angeles International Airport for boarding, an airline employee promptly informed us that said boarding wouldn't happen without negative coronavirus swab tests for all, as required by Taiwan.

"But how can we do that in time for our flight?" I demanded, verging on panic.

"No worries," the smiling employee replied. "There's a 24-hour Urgent Care nearby."

And so, leaving our considerable baggage guarded by a willing accomplice, we raced over to the place by cab, stood in line for an hour to pay $600 US for four swabs, then raced back in time to receive the results by text just as the ticketing agent was preparing to turn us away. Bottom line: we were literally the last passengers to board.

Ah, but here we are in lovely Surigao City relaxing on the lower floors. Well, lovely might be a slight overstatement; even this long after the typhoon, the town is still showing scars. Buildings sit in shambles or in various states of disrepair; piles of debris lie where they were discarded by their owners or the storm; and formerly lush jungles, once adorned by green trees, now stand shamefully naked for all to see.

"Wow," my wife joked yesterday as we drove home from the terminal where the ferry had deposited us. "I like this new view. You can even see the ocean!"

Our positive mood changed the moment we reached the house. Or, perhaps I should say, what was left of it. No, that's an exaggeration; the house is still there. In fact, to be fair, the new roof is almost finished, several rooms have new ceilings and light fixtures, and we finally have electricity after five months of darkness.

Everything else borders on chaos. The building is surrounded by trash piles containing the debris of our previous lives. It's not all bad: an antique typewriter I thought was destroyed is actually only severely damaged. A collection of books signed by their authors remains intact, though thoroughly molded and watermarked. And some of our prized mementos and pieces of art may yet prove to be salvageable.

Mostly, though, it's all either damaged beyond repair or entirely gone. A stroll through the grounds of our property is now an exercise in discovery. This morning, Ivy found the inscribed metal plate commemorating my very first journalism award in 1981. For 40 years, it stayed proudly attached to a handsome wooden plaque; now it's a bent and corroded piece of steel writhing in the dust beneath our feet. And just imagine, yesterday I came across our old copy of Dr. Seuss' *Green Eggs and Ham,* once my son's favorite book, now perfectly preserved in the anarchy of our front yard.

Eventually, we will salvage what we can and discard the rest. We will buy new furniture, organize the house, and complete the final repairs. In time, we will gather new mementos and art to decorate the walls in accordance with our travels and tastes.

And one day the house will be finished. Again.

Until then, I suppose, we'll just have to languish on its lower levels. Have no fear, we've done it before.

PARADISE RE-RECLAIMED

There was good news and bad news on our first return to Siargao Island in the wake of Typhoon Odette.

The bad news was that the storm devastated much of the island, including our little nipa cabin at Magpupungko Beach which got crushed by a fallen tree. The good news? The typhoon also destroyed a hideous wall built by the local municipality that we'd been itching to tear down for years.

The obvious conclusion: nature's on our side, at least regarding the wall. All that's left now is the cleanup.

The verdict is similarly mixed elsewhere on the island, controlled chaos amidst signs of a burgeoning rebirth. General Luna's iconic Cloud 9 Pier, on which I proposed to my wife in 2006, is literally gone with the wind. And all that's left of our favorite coffee shop is a broken and hollowed-out shell.

Ah, but the chaos is pierced regularly by the sounds of hammers and saws. The pier, long a symbol of the island's many charms, is slowly being rebuilt. New lush growth is gradually replacing the vast swaths of jungle torn away by the furious wind. And tourists—including a growing stream of foreigners—are slowly reappearing.

There's also a sullen sadness running through this otherwise hopeful daily re-creation. The emerging salvation is still ragged and torn; not yet entirely whole. On our first day back, we learned that one of Ivy's cousins was feeling suicidal. Financially and emotionally drained by the pandemic and ensuing storm, she had come dangerously close to making a dramatic, if heartbreaking, exit.

But Ivy talked to her, as did many others. And two days later, the wayward cousin showed up at a family reunion bearing a tentative smile and ready, at least on that day, to keep marching on.

There is still, of course, the lingering sadness of all that was lost. Like the little bamboo hut we built during our courtship on a stretch of white sand once owned by Ivy's grandfather. It was just a crude wooden shelter with hearts carved in its ceiling proclaiming our love, now blown to the seven sacred seas. We built it, in fact, on the same trip I proposed to my wife at the end of that famous now-gone pier.

For me, the main takeaway is the astounding optimism and resilience of these Filipino islanders, a quality for which they are widely known. Two years ago, I described the reclamation of Siargao Island in the absence of would-be tourists grounded elsewhere by the raging pandemic.

I remember it well. The water was as crystal clear as I'd ever seen it. Just beneath the surface, a swarm of green fish scurried about while scads of purple crabs crawled past each other on the rocks overhead. But the telltale sign was the smell; instead of sunscreen, the tidepool exuded the natural odor of, yes, the teeming reef that God had intended.

The other day we took another dip in Siargao's miraculous saltwater pool under the famous boulder known as "squatting rock." The rebirth was still apparent, even with—perhaps *because of*—the gawking gaggle of newbies. "This island is amazing," a young visitor from The Netherlands enthusiastically proclaimed. "Everyone is so warm and welcoming. I love the way they smile."

And so it remains; overpowering the reckless pain of uncertainty, the legendary Filipino smile of resilient optimism still shines. It's a smile from which all of us should learn and take heart.

ANOTHER DAY OFF

The silence was unsettling.

On a Monday morning usually given to the strangely soothing sounds of hammers crunching nails, saws biting wood and the indecipherable yet reassuring repartee of construction workers embarking on a day of labor, an almost eerie quiet lurked. This day was different; instead of hammers and saws, only the distant braying of dogs disturbed the morning's uncanny calm.

That's how I started an essay back in 2019 exploring what I perceived as a cultural quirk in countries heavily influenced by Hispanic customs, as is the Philippines. I entitled the piece "Mañana," the Spanish word for *tomorrow*.

It was a trying time for us. After months of waiting, my family and I had finally moved onto the lower levels of the house we were building in Surigao City. But, as we soon discovered, the construction was far from complete. And so we hunkered down, crouching in the basement, anxiously waiting for the job to be completed. Bottom line: what was supposed to take one year took almost five due, in part, to the penchant of Filipino construction workers for taking long unannounced vacations.

"It's like this," the crew's foreman later explained. "In the Philippines, if you have a sack of rice, you stay home. Only when the sack is empty do you go to work."

So you can imagine my consternation upon learning that the Philippine government is considering the implementation of a four-day workweek nationwide. “We should try conserving our energy,” Karl Chua, chief of the National Economic Development Authority, said in a public appearance last month.

While the federal government lacks authority to impose such scheduling restrictions on private companies, officials say, they very well could strongly recommend replacing the current five-day week with four 10-hour days.

Among other things, Chua said, that would allow employees—many of whom worked from home through the COVID pandemic—to “save up because they won’t have to commute every day. This will help us manage the economy.”

To be fair, a four-day workweek offers certain benefits. Workers at companies that have tried it routinely report less stress, better home/work integration and more time for personal endeavors. Some firms have also claimed better employee engagement and increased productivity, though that experience is not universal.

I can vouch for some of those benefits myself; as a *Los Angeles Times* reporter in the late 1990s, I spent several years working a four-day night shift that I still remember with fondness.

There is one area, though, with decidedly mixed results for shortened workweeks: customer satisfaction. While some companies claim to have solved that problem with radically re-jiggered and overlapping schedules, the customers of others have simply gone begging.

That certainly describes my experience during the aforementioned construction of our house. Back then, I rationalized it as the product of a culture valuing life over work.

Many Americans would argue that their Puritan work ethic vs. mañana culture is one reason the USA has consistently provided such a high standard of living for so many while the Philippines is still, well, a developing country.

But that's not all bad. While surveys consistently rank Filipinos among the world's happiest and friendliest people, Americans are better known for their high levels of stress and depression, disintegrating families, addiction to work, alienation from society and each other, mass violence, annoying outspokenness and impatient, demanding personalities. Bottom line: like most things in life, it's complicated.

But that was then. Now I find myself in a weird *Déjà vu.* Typhoon Odette wreaked utter havoc on our still-shiny new home, blowing off its roof and destroying all its windows, ceilings and doors. We have hired a crew to repair the damage, but their progress is, once again, achingly slow.

It pains me to say this, but the last thing they need is another day off.

RECONNECTING

It started as a tiny niggle, I wrote back in 2018 shortly after moving into our then-under-construction house in a remote barangay of Surigao City.

The niggle developed into a source of deep existential angst over the lack of a decent internet signal. “No internet?” I whined. We’d be completely disconnected. Not only from friends and family, but from the larger world outside. Without a proper internet signal, how would we survive?

Eventually I solved the problem, for a time anyway, by regularly visiting a coffee shop downtown that offered a serviceable connection. For the price of a latte, I discovered, I could surf the web at my leisure, a solution that lasted for nearly a year.

Then Globe gifted us with its saintly smile. The same company that, along with Smart and PLDT, had flatly refused earlier entreaties to serve our sparsely populated corner of Mindanao, now duly anointed us with a plan that, despite frequent interruptions and slowdowns, at least kept us hanging online.

Until Typhoon Odette changed everything.

Ah, but recently we heard some encouraging news: Bongbong Marcos Jr., the new president, it seems, is planning to vastly improve Mindanao’s internet connection with the help of billionaire Elon Musk’s Starlink satellite communications network. Soon, Information and Communication Secretary Ivan

John Uy told *The Manila Times*, "we can provide free high-speed internet access to our geographically isolated and disadvantaged areas in the Philippines, ensuring that no Filipino will get left behind."

Because it uses low-orbit satellites, he explained, Starlink can easily establish strong connections in areas where a dearth of paying customers discourages other companies from setting up what he called "missionary routes."

Areas like our own Punta Bilar.

Which is why we were surprised to receive an unscheduled visit from a representative of PLDT. The company, she explained, had recently wired our area for fiber optic internet; would we care to partake?

"Are you here because of all the times I left you my phone number last year?" I immediately wanted to know.

In fact, I had visited their local office downtown frequently only to be told that the fiber optic wiring would be completed in a "week or two" and I would certainly be among the first to know. Eventually, I gave up and stopped making my biweekly visits.

"I don't have your phone number at all, sir," she said cheerfully, deflating my ego in an instant. "I'm just surveying the area for potential customers."

Because word on the street has it that Musk's satellite system won't be available until sometime next year, we quickly lunged at the thin fiber of optic hope this smiling woman was dangling before us. That was two weeks ago. Now, if the installer would just show up...

TROPHY AMERICAN HUSBAND

A kept man.

That's how some of my friends see me. But here's the thing: I don't mind. In fact, I think it's kinda cool. Let me explain.

When Ivy and I got married 15 years ago, we held traditional roles. I worked full time as a newspaper reporter, earning a more-than-adequate salary. And Ivy, a new Philippine immigrant to America, stayed home, maintaining the household, and preparing to launch her career.

Then things got turned upside down. I lost my job, and our first child was born, practically in the same month. Almost simultaneously, Ivy's occupation in the medical field began taking off. And, given that our enormous age gap put me much closer to retirement anyway, we made a prudent decision: Ivy went to work whole hog while I stayed home caring for our dear little Isaac.

Ok, fast forward to the present. Now we reside in the Philippines, where life is considerably less expensive. And, in deference to my still-breathing-though-rapidly-declining masculine ego, let me just say this: it was my life savings that paid for both the house we built here and the one we maintain in Southern California. And too, during much of the year we live comfortably on my somewhat adequate (at least by Philippine standards) Social Security income and newspaper pension.

Ah, but then there are those other months. Like the ones coming up, scarred by the absence of several million pesos spent repairing our home in the wake of the calamitous Typhoon Odette. Or the humongous legal fees paid in an agonizing Siargao Island land dispute we've been fighting now for several years. Not to mention the painful stretch required to pay the growing monthly electric bills for our increasingly buzz-worthy household.

Recently Ivy embarked on her annual pilgrimage to America to spend several months working as a traveling clinical laboratory scientist, for which hospitals pay her obscenely high fees. So, once again, I am reduced to the status of a stay-at-home dad taking care of our boy.

That reality got a big laugh during an appearance once when I explained it this way to a Filipino audience: "We are engaged in a reversal of roles," I said. "My Filipino wife in America sends money to her American husband in the Philippines."

Boy, what a roar! Because it doesn't usually go that way, does it? Mostly it's the other way around. Which fits perfectly into the "reverse diaspora" theme I was pushing for the new book I was hoping they'd buy.

"I think the feminists in the crowd really loved that line," my publicist later gushed.

I must sheepishly admit, however, to not being overly enamored of my newly retrieved designation as a trophy husband. A trophy wife, of course, is defined by Wikipedia as "a young, attractive wife regarded as a status symbol for an older man." Trophy husbands are a bit more complicated: "A younger, attractive man in a relationship with an older, wealthier person?" Nope! Or, how about this: "The partner of a narcissist who's only around to boost a narcissist's ego?" Nope, nope, nope!!

Ah, but here's one that sort of applies: "A trophy husband can also refer to a stay-at-home dad." Or, as they call them in Sweden, a "latte papa."

And so, we circle back to where we started more than a decade ago. Isaac is now a pre-teen, which makes me fear that serving as a trophy husband may soon prove far more difficult than being a clinical laboratory scientist.

I'm thinking of asking Ivy for another reversal of roles.

GLOBE AT HOME: NO ESCAPE

It seemed like a good idea at the time.

In fact, it was the *only* idea because none of the country's other internet providers dared venture into our sparsely populated barangay, where, frankly, they were unlikely to get rich.

So we settled for Globe at Home wi-fi which, for a while, provided internet service that usually worked, mostly at speeds almost adequate for our needs. Like an awful marriage, we settled in for the long haul, convincing ourselves that the relationship would improve over time.

But, alas, things got no better. Then Typhoon Odette knocked out the power, rendering our modem inoperable. And so, acting from the US where we were trapped for an indefinite period, we made our first attempt to ask Globe for a divorce, or at least a legal separation. I spent hours on the company's website searching for a means of escape. Finding none, I then lobbed a forlorn email message into the company's cyberspace, begging to be shown the door. And when that didn't work, we enlisted the services of my wife's sister—still stuck at the Philippine house with no signal—to make an in-person call.

"Sorry," she told us the next day, or words to that effect, "they say you have to go there yourself." And so, assuming—naively it turns out—that some accommodation would be made for victims of the typhoon, we tabled the issue pending our eventual return.

So you can imagine my surprise when, back in Surigao eight months later, the company that had partnered us in life now welcomed us with determined indifference. "Sure you can disconnect," the Globe guy said, "but you have to put it in writing after settling your bill."

By which he meant dishing out enough cash to cover the two months without internet for which we were in arrears, notwithstanding the six months without internet for which we had already paid. Clearly, all other exits were barred. So, we reluctantly made good on the tab while my wife, whose name the account bore, drafted and signed a letter requesting its immediate dissolution. Then she flew back to California for a three-month work assignment to help pay for the costly Odette repairs.

Which is why I was shocked a few weeks later upon receiving yet another bill for the daunting internet connection that refused to acknowledge its own death. This time, I marched straight down to the office myself. "Don't you have the letter my wife signed?" I asked incredulously. "What happened, did you lose it?"

The Globe guy smiled beneficently, waiting for me to calm down. "No sir," he said finally, still sporting that annoying grin. "We have your wife's letter but couldn't reach her to confirm."

By now, I was seeing red.

"Waitaminute," I said. "You're telling me we're still getting bills because my wife didn't answer her phone?"

"We tried calling twice," he offered helpfully.

"Look," I said, trying hard to maintain my composure. "She is abroad and has received no phone calls or messages. You have her written cancellation request, which she signed right here in your presence. I'm her husband and, speaking on her behalf, I'm asking you to honor that request."

"Oh, so sorry, sir," the young man said pleasantly. "We are just a franchise without that authority."

And so I gave up.

Several weeks have now passed, and we've embarked on a new fling with a company called PLDT, which, so far, has treated us quite well. And what of our ex-partner, the bitterly possessive Globe at Home? Like spurned spouses everywhere, it continues harassing us, specifically in monthly statements chronicling our increasing debt. Fortunately, we have learned to ignore them. For we have detached emotionally and are finally moving on.

Our fondest hope is that one day the annoying Globe at Home will do the same.

MAGIC CHIMES

Let's just say it's been a difficult 12 months.

A year after Typhoon Odette and following gargantuan efforts that have cost several million pesos, we are finally approaching recovery. Just in time for the power to go out again, an electrical short to burn a hole in our newly lacquered wooden floor, a water dispenser to spring a leak emptying its liquid contents onto that same floor, and my personal computer to completely blow up. Oh yes, and the door of the upstairs bathroom to break down locking my son inside requiring us to saw off its knobs.

And all that happened just last week.

"Oh my God," I moaned to our live-in driver, cook, maintenance person and female helper, Brad. "What the hell is going on?"

Brad just smiled knowingly, and then sadly sighed. "It's because of how the doors are placed," she explained patiently, as if talking to a child. "We Filipinos believe that if you build doors facing each other, evil enters through one while your money exits through the other. Several of our workers have commented on it."

Oh great, I thought, *now* she tells me.

Here's where I must make a painful confession; I'm not immune to the seductions of superstition. After completing the construction of our house a few years ago, in fact, we followed the Filipino custom of inviting a local priest to bless it throughout with a generous sprinkling of holy water. And, to improve our odds of good fortune by covering all the bases, we also attached to its doorpost a small Israeli *mezuzah* containing Judaism's declaration of faith to bless and protect all who entered.

Would it hiss and explode when touched by the sacred moisture about to be imbued by this Catholic man of Jesus? Would hot steam fill the room as the flames of Hell burned our new house to the ground?

Fortunately, none of that happened. But neither did the mezuzah provide much protection; a week later, the World Health Organization declared a global pandemic and, 21 months after that, Category Six Super Typhoon Odette blew that tiny Jewish arc far away and out of sight, presumably to rest with the remains of all our other slaughtered belongings.

"OK," I said to Brad, getting serious now, "so what can we do about those doors?"

Turns out you need to block them with fresh orchids and lotus blossoms, according to Chinese/Filipino lore. Or, lacking those hard-to-find items, mere pictures of same will do. Which is how I ended up spending several hours last week googling "pictures of orchids and lotus blossoms," to no avail.

Ah, but my housekeeper/driver/cook/handyman/now-turned-*guru*, Brad, has another idea. "How about," she suggested, "we use *Feng Shui* magic wind chimes? I think they should do the trick."

And so we are searching for some online.

The term *Feng Shui*, apparently, is derived from two Chinese words – "feng," meaning wind, and "shui," meaning water—suggesting that human life should flow in harmony with its surroundings. By definition, therefore, *Feng Shui*, according to one source, is "a practice of arranging the pieces in living spaces to create balance with the natural world. This is what it means to *Feng Shui* your home."

All of which makes perfect sense to *me*. I support anything that will stop the escape of our hard-earned cash through that infernal second door.

OUR TREMBLING HOUSE

Our house gets the shakes almost daily.

It usually happens in the middle of the night when the world is sleeping and the atmosphere is still. Suddenly, a violent gust of wind smashes into a wall, making the windows rattle and the rafters complain. The blows are so powerful that the air literally howls, as if moaning in pain. Then—in minutes, hours, or days—the threat departs and tranquility remains.

I never used to notice the wind that now startles me awake each night. So I mentioned it to Brad, our helpmate who has lived here longer than I. "Is it climate change?" I wanted to know. "Because I don't remember the wind ever blowing this strong."

Brad thought for a moment before replying. Then explained that, though climate change may be a factor, the main reason we're feeling the ultra-strong winds routinely these days is because Typhoon Odette scattered the trees that once sheltered our house. Not to mention that, even as we spoke, another Category Five typhoon—this one called Noru—was preparing to make landfall up north in Luzon.

Recently, a tremor of another kind threatened to disrupt our lives. A man I never heard of summoned me to a meeting at barangay headquarters to declare that the lot we purchased in 2013 is actually his. Seems he's related to the now-deceased farmer from whom we bought it and who, he believes, cheated him out of his portion. Such claims are not uncommon in the

Philippines, where landowners are legally required to divide their holdings equally among all rightful heirs.

"Clearly your quarrel is not with us," retorted Jake Miranda, the friend and prominent Surigaonon, who helped us acquire the land and now spoke on my behalf. Later, he—as well as several others—assured me that the man's claim has almost no chance of succeeding.

And yet it reminded me of something I have always secretly known; that things seeming permanent can sometimes be fragile. While that's true virtually everywhere on earth, it is especially clear here in the Philippines where typhoons and land disputes seem to abound. We argue and cajole and love and grasp, both in ecstasy and in pain. But one day those arguments cease and only the trembling house remains. Life on these islands is close to the core. And so we shake, whisper and moan, always reaching for the light just beyond an invisible door.

Which brings to mind a piece of writing by Albert Camus, the famous French philosopher, author, dramatist, and journalist who won the Nobel Prize in Literature for 1957 just three years before dying at 47.

In the midst of hate, he wrote, *I found there was, within me, an invincible love. In the midst of tears, I found there was, within me, an invincible smile. In the midst of chaos, I found there was, within me, an invincible calm. I realized, through it all, that in the midst of winter, I found there was, within me, an invincible summer. And that makes me happy. For it says that no matter how hard the world pushes against me, within me, there's something stronger—something better, pushing right back.*

I pray our own resilience will persist in the house that now trembles.

4.
CULTURE

TIKTOKING TEENS

It became an almost weekly occurrence at our house in Surigao City.

My teenage nieces would gather somewhere on the property to produce a TikTok video for their followers online. Working in small groups or alone, they would choreograph dance routines compatible with whatever music they'd selected. Then, as their chosen tune blared loudly from Bluetooth speakers, they'd dance their hearts out, grinning widely with pageantry and pleasure. And I'd feel sated knowing these beloved young people were enjoying just being themselves.

It was only later, seeing the finished products online, that I experienced occasional heart attacks. Though it wasn't always there, it happened frequently enough to make an impression; a highly visible eroticism I'd never noticed in person.

"Listen to my heart," declared the caption in one production, highlighting the wildly suggestive moves of an otherwise innocent youngster.

A *Wall Street Journal* article decried the psychological damage potentially inflicted on teenagers—especially girls—seduced by the lure of openly exhibiting eroticism online. "I wanted to get famous on TikTok," Julia Anderson, now 18, told the newspaper. "And I learned that if you post stuff showing your body, people will start liking it."

The problem, according to the psychologist who eventually treated her for anxiety and depression, is that such early exposure can warp a youngster's self-esteem. "For a young girl who's developing her identity to be swept up into a sexual world like that is hugely destructive," therapist Paul Sunsert said. "When teen girls are rewarded for their sexuality, they come to believe that their only value is in how they look."

Another psychologist said of one 16-year-old client: "The more likes she had, the more revealing her outfits became."

Eventually, the girl ended up chatting with an older man who persuaded her to take their conversations offline and into a messaging app. She had already sent him several partially nude photos of herself and was making plans to meet in person when her parents, discovering the texts, called a halt to the burgeoning and likely destructive relationship.

"When you combine human behavior and algorithms," her therapist said, "things get messy. We're trying to clean it up, one client at a time."

I have no reason to believe that any of this happened to my lovely Filipino nieces. Most of them are in their early 20s now and, as far as I can tell, showing no signs of discomfort or distress. But what struck me then and strikes me today is the vast difference between some young women's online and in-person personas. Face-to-face in close physical proximity, they seem like sweet, reticent, poised and innocent young ladies. Put them in front of a webcam, though, and a whole new personality quickly emerges.

"To us, she's this sweet girl," Julia's parents told the *Journal*. "So, it's almost like this split personality between who she really is and how she portrayed herself on TikTok. When we confronted her about it, she was like, 'Mom, that's what everyone is doing.'"

My youngest daughter is not quite five. My fondest hope for both of us is that, by the time she's a teenager, TikTok will be long gone.

MAIL-ORDER BRIDES

The tropes were familiar in the early days of our marriage.

People said we had hooked up so Ivy could get a green card. Or that I was trading on my white privilege for a sexy Filipino bride. One of them even found its way into a newspaper following my account of romance across the sea.

"David Haldane Has a Mail-Order Bride and Wants His Neighbors to Be Cool With It," read a headline in the *Orange County Weekly*, a then-widely-read Southern California-based publication.

And there it was, the phrase I'd come to detest, the so-called *mail-order bride*. In the years that followed, I talked and wrote a lot about that. About how there was no longer any such thing. And how the myth of the mail-order bride had become a cudgel with which to discredit relationships such as ours.

Now I'm not so sure. The reason for my uncertainty: the news that four Philippine nationals in Los Angeles are going to prison for, well, providing mail-order brides.

Here's how it worked. Marcialito Biol Benitez, 50, would procure clients from around the world wishing to enter the United States illegally. Then he'd match them with US citizens willing to pose as their husbands or wives.

From October 2016 to March 2022, authorities say, Benitez and three accomplices set up 600 phony weddings, netting $8 million by charging clients $20,000 to $30,000 each. "It's the utmost honor and privilege to become an American citizen,"

Jodi Cohen, a special agent with the FBI, declared, yet the conspirators "made an absolute sham of that process."

Among the services provided: assessing whether make-believe couples had enough "good chemistry" to fool immigration officials; counseling them on how to ace interviews by memorizing "spousal" details; and helping them shop for matching clothing. In addition, the fraudulent matchmakers would help prepare phony documents, provide wedding chapels that wouldn't confirm whether the marriages were real, decorate those chapels with props, and document the wedding ceremonies with photos.

Following the fake weddings, the marriage pretenders would provide addresses simulating cohabitation and offer help in registering vehicles, opening joint bank accounts, filing joint tax returns, and purchasing life insurance policies. They would also keep paid partners available should future complications arise.

Ah, but then they got caught. Earlier this year, Benitez was sentenced to 22 months in prison followed by three years of supervised release. A co-defendant, Engilbert Ulan, 43, received a prison sentence of 14 months while two others—Juanita Pacson, 48, and Nino Valmeo, 47—were confined to home arrests of four and six months, respectively.

Their sentences would have been harsher in the Philippines. Here, under a law called the "Anti-Mail Order Spouse Act," anyone guilty of engaging in a money-making scheme aimed at "matching or offering...a Filipino to a foreign national for marriage" is subject to 15 years in prison plus a fine of up to a million pesos (nearly $18,000 US). If the crime is committed by a syndicate or "on a large scale," according to the law, the sentence is increased to 20 years, plus a fine of up to *five* million (more than $88,000 US).

And yet such practices continue. In 2024, the Philippine Bureau of Immigration intercepted several Filipinas attempting to leave the country with fake Chinese or Korean husbands.

"Most of the victims here are those looking for a job [abroad]," Immigration Deputy spokesman Melvin Mabulac said in a public briefing reported by *The Manila Times*. "They are looking for a [fast] way out, evading the Department of Migrant Workers."

One case, the paper reported, involved a woman who "endured verbal and physical abuse from her pseudo husband, who demanded payment for her food and repeatedly threatened to kill her whenever she resisted having sex with him."

All of which, of course, makes life harder for genuine transnational couples like us and our friends. So, to those seeking love across the waters, let me just say this: be honest, be careful, be strong.

Regarding my own 17-year marriage, I have but one thing to add: thank God we did it in an earlier, more innocent time.

BELIEVING IN GOD AND SANTA CLAUS

A few days ago, my 11-year-old son asked a terrifying question. "Is Santa Claus real?" Isaac wanted to know.

It's a question I'd been dreading. Though we have continued our annual family ritual of hanging Christmas stockings above the mantel and leaving cookies and milk out for the jolly fat man's consumption, both my wife and I have, for some time now, suspected young Isaac was getting wise.

That doubt was probably hastened by our move to the Philippines, where Christmas is a serious religious event with little space for silly fantasies involving a fat man dressed in red pajamas. In fact, there are no chimneys here in the tropics, so how the heck would he get in anyway? And the idea of a bag full of presents runs counter to a national character comprising large doses of modesty, faith, and self-sacrifice. Not to mention, of course, widespread poverty and unrestrained procreation preventing many families from partaking in any sort of expansive gift-giving at all.

No, in the Philippines Christmas is mostly a solemn recognition and celebration of the birthday of Jesus expressed by roaming Christmas carolers at the doors of relatives, friends, and neighbors. As well as lots of praying, churchgoing, and ardent religiosity in its various forms.

And yet this was the first time Isaac had given voice to any doubts, so the question was anything but casual. Perhaps our dear little American-born son was finally becoming Filipino.

I paused for a stressful few seconds to ponder. Then came up with the only answer I could think of. "Santa is real," I told my son, "if you believe in him." Apparently satisfied, Isaac went on with his day.

A recent essay in the *New York Times* reminded me of that conversation. Under the headline "How to Pray to a God You Don't Believe In," Scott Hershovitz, a professor of law and philosophy at the University of Michigan, recalls a similar conversation with his own son regarding God which, the professor says, reframed his view of religion.

"Is God real?" the son asked when he was only four.

"What do *you* think?" Hershovitz replied.

"I think that for real God is pretend and for pretend God is real," the little boy announced.

"What do you mean?" the stunned professor asked.

"God isn't real," the boy said. "But when we pretend, he *is*."

That wise young one's logic pretty much sums up my own sentiments regarding the alleged Supreme Being. When asked, I usually describe myself as an agnostic, i.e. someone who doesn't truly know whether or not there's a God. In fact, I often say, I'm not sure God's existence is verifiably knowable by any living human being. After all, I argue, if there is a good and omniscient God, how can he permit all the darkness and pain we see in the world?

Ah, but that's my brain speaking; the rational, fact-based, mind space we call intellect. In truth, there's a whole other part; the emotional, intuitive, subjective space some call soul. And in that world, for me anyway, God is very much present. I feel him while watching a beautiful sunset, hearing a beloved piece of music, or gazing into the eyes of my children. I frequently refer to him by name, both in conversation and in writing. Sometimes I even pray to him during difficult times.

Do I really believe God will hear my prayers and save me from impending disasters, mishaps, and agonies? Hardly. What

I do hope, though, is that pretending he is real—*believing* in him—will give me the wisdom, courage, and fortitude to better navigate those troubled waters myself.

"He doesn't care about pleasure and pain," Professor Hershovitz writes of God in his essay. "He cares about what pleasure and pain make possible—compassion, redemption, and heroic acts..."

Yesterday, Isaac let me know he had resolved his doubts about Santa. "I've decided I believe in him," my sweet son said. "That way I'll get presents at Christmastime. If you don't believe in Santa, you just get coal."

Oh well, I guess he's still an American at heart after all. From the mouths of babes, into my heart and soul.

SAVING ROOSTERS

What struck me most was how quickly it ended.

One minute, two healthy roosters strutted about, looking threatening and robust. Then, boom, after a ferocious instant of combat, one lay dead while the other accepted the proud strokes of its master.

Hmm, not unlike life itself, I mused, not for the last time.

We had happened on the scene while driving down a remote road of Siargao Island. The first thing I noticed was a horde of motorcycles parked by what looked like a bamboo hut without walls.

"Hey, what's going on?" I asked my wife, who hails from these parts.

"Oh, nothing," she shrugged matter-of-factly. "Probably just a cockfight."

"Really?" I gasped. "Oh my God, I've never seen one. Can we stop?"

And so I found myself needling through a mostly male crowd for a front-row view of this perennial struggle between life and death.

There's something fascinating about watching a living thing die before your eyes. I'd first noticed it years before at a bullfight in Mexico. There he was, a gigantic fierce-looking red beast trying its best to subjugate the taunting human before him. Everyone knew, of course, the eventual outcome. And yet that big bull never gave up, never wavered, just kept attacking until he could attack no more.

When it was all over and the beast's bloody carcass lay humbled in the dirt, I reflected on the gleams of satisfaction in nearly every watcher's eye. Mexico, like the Philippines, is a poor country where life is difficult and sometimes cruel. Perhaps, it occurred to me, this dramatic re-enactment of the life-and-death struggle inspired in its audience a sense of victory over the deadly forces of nature, the illusion of ultimate human triumph over that which brings life down.

Philippine cockfights, of course, differ in a major way: one rooster survives while another—its defeated competitor—ends up dead in the dust. Instead of pitting man against nature, it seems, the cockfight pits nature against itself or—with roosters standing in for people—man against man. Is this, I wonder, a more realistic depiction of life as most of us experience it, populated by winners and losers?

I thought of that recently after reading a dispatch from America where, predictably, both bullfighting *and* cockfighting are strictly prohibited. Predictable because, in a relatively prosperous country like the USA, average people don't live as close to the daily struggle for survival as in Mexico and the Philippines. And because, frankly, they don't like being reminded of it.

The story came out of Jurupa Valley, California, where, according to the *Los Angeles Times*, authorities raided a cockfight at a private residence attended by more than 200 people, most of whom fled. The renegade homeowner wasn't so lucky: besides citing him for illegally possessing fighting blades worn by the combatant birds, the Department of Animal Services—tasked with overseeing the wellbeing of non-humans—was pursuing felony animal cruelty charges against this hapless lover of gore.

And what of the 143 roosters they found in his barn?

Those cocks "are bred to be fighting birds," a spokesman explained, "so you can't... put them on a farm." The obvious solution: "humanely" kill all of them, a process that took the entire night.

Too bad those quarrelsome roosters weren't in the Philippines, where at least half of them would have survived. A fitting representation, perhaps, of our uncertain lives.

MY SALAD LIFE

Quinoa Salad.

That's what the menu said. I was surprised and flummoxed because I honestly thought I knew every kind of salad there was, and I certainly hadn't heard of this one. "What's quinoa?" I asked the woman behind the counter at the Green Waves Café in Siargao Island's notoriously hip town of General Luna.

"Oh," she said, "we also have a green salad."

"Yes, but what's quinoa?"

"Oh," she said again, "well, that salad has lettuce, chickpea, tomato, basil, apple, balsamic vinaigrette and, of course, quinoa."

"You're not understanding me," I insisted, trying to be patient. "What, exactly, is quinoa?"

"Oh," she said for the third time, now looking somewhat flummoxed herself. There followed a long discussion involving several employees in a language I didn't understand. "It's a kind of bean," one of them finally piped up.

Now it was my turn to say "oh." Then I ordered the damn thing to find out what it was for myself.

Salads and I go way back. As a child I ate lots of them made with lettuce and white Miracle Whip dressing. It was one of the few things my immigrant German Jewish mother could hustle down my throat. "Eat more!" she would insist in the way of mothers everywhere.

"Leave him alone," my father always responded. "When he gets hungry, he will eat."

The strange thing was that I never got hungry enough to eat much of anything that wasn't green. Which is why I'm often viewed with bewilderment here in the Philippines, where fish and meat are king. "He's a lettuce eater!" I've heard more than one Filipino mutter under his or her breath. Before I got them properly trained, some of my relatives even dreaded having me over for dinner. "But what will we feed him?" my distraught mother-in-law once asked my wife after learning that I would be at their table. "We have no food!"

In recent years, my relationship with salads has sometimes turned wobbly. Back in 2018, one got named after me at a startup restaurant in Surigao City that was trying to attract foreign customers. For me, it was a moment of unprecedented pride. Then, two weeks later, another salad put me in the hospital for several days with an extremely nasty intestinal amoeba.

Perhaps sharing your name with a salad is kind of like a marriage. Being unfaithful can cause a calamity.

Since then, I've changed my ways and would never even think of two-timing my steady salad. Which is why I seldom eat one outside the confines of home. Except, perhaps, one as provocative and tempting as Quinoa.

Turns out it's a flowering South American plant with edible seeds rich in protein, dietary fiber and B vitamins. So I closed my eyes and gobbled it down quickly, hoping my infidelity would go unnoticed.

Despite such occasional indiscretions, however, the situation at home is getting better. My Filipino family now serves me at least two salads daily without even being asked. And, indeed, the global status of the green stuff seems to finally be improving.

An August 2022 *Wall Street Journal* story ran under the headline “McDonald’s Customers Love Salads—Who Knew?” When the company famous for hamburgers stopped offering salads at the beginning of the pandemic, the *Journal* reported, “many restaurant operators rejoiced. The hand-assembled mélange of greens was cumbersome to make. Diners wouldn’t miss it, they thought, as they imposed the menu change.”

Much to their astonishment, however, many diners missed it *a lot*. “McDonald’s very much has lost me,” one of them told the newspaper. And tens of thousands converged on Twitter to demand that salads return.

“Who knew,” the *Journal* concluded, that “some of the throngs going to McDonald’s every day were there for the lettuce?”

The mania is even spreading to the Philippines where my sister-in-law, without being prodded, recently asked for her very own helping of the green stuff. “I think it must be healthy,” she announced.

Hallelujah, I thought, *God is good*!

SPEAKING ENGLISH IN THE PHILIPPINES

It's both a blessing and a curse. A double-edged-sword, as they say, a blade that cuts both ways.

What I'm talking about is being a native English speaker in the Philippines.

The good thing about it, of course, is that most Filipinos speak English. The bad thing? Just that, well, most Filipinos speak English.

Let me explain.

Growing up in an English-speaking country like the US, as I did, significantly decreases one's chances of ever learning another language. Why? Because practically everyone in the world speaks your native tongue. Which, I can attest from personal experience, dramatically undermines your propensity and motivation to learn a foreign language.

It's not that I haven't tried. Shortly after arriving in this luscious island nation, I spent several thousand pesos on a self-directed online course promising to teach me Bisaya, the native language of the Northern Mindanao province in which I live. And I worked on it, I really did. So hard that I was able to complete the first lesson 19 times. The problem was that I could never get to lesson two.

Believe me, that's not something I'm proud of.

And so I did what many expats here do, resigned myself to picking up whatever I could from conversations with the locals. Unfortunately, that turned out to be almost nothing. Because those who felt confident in their English routinely insisted on speaking to me in the only language I already knew. And those who didn't—which included most of my Filipino wife's immediate family—just refrained from speaking to me at all. Until eventually, I gave up on the notion of bilingualism, resigning myself to living in my own private mono linguistic world.

Ah, but last year I got a chance to redeem myself. That's when my adult daughter and I journeyed to Germany, where my mother was born. Being the son of a native German, I had studied that language in school. And during a brief sojourn in Berlin 54 years ago, even mastered it sufficiently enough to sustain a six-month romantic relationship with a young woman named Krystal who couldn't speak a word of English.

I mean, pretty impressive, *nicht wahr*?

Nein!!!!

Translation: No way.

Because Germany has changed a great deal since 1970. Mainly in that, almost without exception, everyone there now speaks English. Which meant that they were generally better at my language than I was at theirs. Which also meant that any chance for self-redemption in the eyes of my extremely bright and talented daughter was gone with the wind.

Kind of like in the Philippines.

A 2024 study conducted by Education First, an international education company specializing in language training actually ranked Berlin among the world's top ten cities in English proficiency. And as for countries, well, the Philippines ranked 20th, up from 22nd the year before.

"English is the language of global commerce and culture," concluded an editorial reporting on the study in *The Manila*

Times. "It will be to our peril if we diminish one of the few advantages we have over the rest of the world."

There are times and places, of course, that, despite everything I've said, I would gladly give my left kidney for someone to speak my language. The last time that happened was five years ago, during a 14-hour layover in China with my then-eight-year-old son.

"I'm thirsty," Isaac announced after our 3 a.m. landing at the Chongqing airport.

Ordinarily, of course, that wouldn't pose a major problem. But this was China, where water can only be purchased with local currency, Visa cards are not accepted, and no one speaks English nor cares to communicate with foreigners who do.

Suffice it to say, it was an extremely long night.

Now safely back in the Philippines, I've surrendered the notion of ever becoming fluent in another language. Except maybe the universal language of Tanduay rum.

ACHING TESTICLES

It was 3 a.m. and my patience was waning.

I had come to Surigao City's St. Paul Medical Center to see about, well... a persistent pain in my left testicle. But now I'd been waiting in line for almost five hours and was feeling increasingly annoyed.

"Jesus," I snapped at my sister-in-law, who'd graciously consented to accompany me. "This is bordering on absurd!"

The thing is, it wasn't an emergency room doc I was waiting to see, but a highly recommended urologist who maintained regular office hours. The problem was that they started at 10 p.m. and didn't end until he'd seen all his patients.

"Just come in at 10," his secretary had cheerfully instructed. "He'll get to you when he can."

Back in the US, the procedure would have been different. The doctor's secretary would have given me an appointment and, even though it might be weeks in advance, I'd have spent those weeks waiting at home rather than in some darkened hospital hallway. And never at 3 a.m.

"OK, that's it," I finally muttered under my breath. I stood up abruptly and shrugged my shoulders for dramatic effect. "I'm done waiting. Let's just boogie on out of here!"

Then, suddenly, as if by magic, the doors of fate opened and enveloped me in their soothing folds. "Sir David Haldane," the assistant called before gently ushering me into a small nondescript office. The doctor, clearly wide awake and far more functional than I felt at that ungodly hour, studied the scrotal ultrasound I had tucked under my arm.

"Oh," he said, and then, "Ah. Well, you don't have cancer, that's for sure. Looks like an infection of the epididymis, the tube connecting the testicle to the vas deferens transporting sperm to the ejaculatory ducts." He quickly drew a diagram to help me understand. "Nothing to worry about," the doctor assured me. "The pain you're feeling is from a cyst. I'll prescribe some pills and in two weeks, you'll be fine."

In truth, I'd heard very little after "you don't have cancer." But I knew I'd been saved. And so, went home to sleep soundly in my bed for the rest of that night and day.

Here's the point: while the practice of medicine in the Philippines is often disorganized and inefficient, it's also extremely competent. More so, in my experience, than in the United States. That reality was driven home to me two weeks later during a second visit to the same doctor who, after discovering a grossly obese prostate residing in my nether regions, scoffed at the medicine I'd been prescribed for it by an American doctor years before. "That stuff will loosen up your bladder," he practically chortled, "but I can give you something that will actually help."

So far, it seems to be doing just that. Which confirms my earlier impressions of Filipino doctors gleaned from once spending three days hospitalized for a nasty intestinal amoeba, later having an ugly assemblage of ear wax removed from my unhearing ears and, finally, vicariously experiencing the birth of a child I'd fathered despite my infection-prone epididymis.

My Filipino wife, who has worked in healthcare both in the Philippines and the United States, thinks the difference has to do with technology. In the US, she says, where medical technology is highly sophisticated and readily available, medical practitioners rely on it more heavily than on their own knowledge and experience.

“When something breaks down,” asserts Ivy, currently serving as a clinical laboratory scientist at two California hospitals during her annual visits to the West Coast, “everybody freaks out and doesn’t know what to do.”

And too, she says, doctors in the Philippines—where they are fewer and farther between – see a much wider variety and number of cases. Which is probably why they keep their patients waiting so long.

But here’s the thing: there are worse experiences in life than spending the night in a long, darkened hallway. Especially if, at its end, you learn that your testicles are good to go.

Bottom line: I would do it all again in a flash without uttering a single complaint. Let’s just hope, though, that I never ever have to.

UBIQUITOUS UBE

I have always had a tenuous relationship with Philippine food.

Mainly, it's an aversion to seafood that has plagued my whole life. I even found a name for it: *ichthyophobia*, which Wikipedia defines as "fear of fish, including fear of eating fish or fear of dead fish." Which is definitely not helpful in a province famed for the seafood of which it is proud.

Nor, being an avid salad-eater with instinctive vegetarian tendencies, have I found much joy in other common Philippine fare. Both *sisig* and *crispy pata*, made respectively from pork cheeks and pig knuckles, leave me uninspired. I'm not a fan of stewed oxtail, cooked mole crickets, or whole frogs stuffed with minced pork. And neither fresh snails cooked in coconut milk nor pig guts stewed in warm pork blood have tempted me to take a bite. You've probably already guessed by now that I also haven't tasted the nation's infamous *balut*, a popular delicacy comprising 17-day-old duck embryos still encased in their shells.

Ah, but local deserts are a whole other thing. Give me a heaping *halo-halo* piled high with shaved ice, banana, garbanzos, milk and ice cream on absolutely any day. A yummy custard *leche flan* is certainly worth dying for. And *ube*, that wonderful purple ingredient infusing local cakes, shakes and creams, has become one of the grand passions of my otherwise uninspired culinary life.

Which is why I'm happy to report that my favorite flavor is about to make its debut on the global stage. At least that's the prediction of *New York Times* food writer Kim Severson, who included the luscious desert on her annual list of edibles about to go viral.

"Ube, a slightly nutty-tasting, vanilla-accented purple yam from the Philippines," she noted, "is showing up on lots of trend lists and in all kinds of foods and drinks, from pies and waffles to lattes and ube coladas. It easily made the list of colors and flavors that capture the mood of 2023."

Other foods on Severson's list include yaupon tea made from American holly trees, as well as avocado-imbued cocktails and deserts. Also, Nigerian *egusi* stew featuring goat, cow skin, mushrooms and seeds, coastal cocktails garnished with crab claws and oysters, plus crispy chicken skins served with nachos and ketchup.

That last item I can see myself indulging in regularly. And I certainly won't mind having an occasional fruit cocktail primed with avocado green.

As for the various *unsweetened* items of nourishment ensconced in the Filipino diet, well, I suppose I'll just have to continue treading lightly. I have no desire, for instance, to revisit an experience encountered four years ago after a fun-loving, face-licking yellow dog named Sandy wandered onto the road in front of our house and got smashed by a car.

"There's good news and bad news," the construction foreman then working on our house announced immediately upon our return from a weekend getaway. "The bad news is that Sandy's dead. The good news is that the workers across the street are having a wonderful dinner."

I turned down their invitation to join.

A FILIPINO WEDDING

The most poignant moment came when the bride danced with her father.

The elderly man had to be helped to the dance floor. Once there, though, the smile on his face glowed with radiance as he steadied himself in her arms. And as they gently swayed to the strains of "Dance with My Father," the emotional swell in my heart could not be stilled. Thus, I recognized once again a major reason I live and love in the Philippines.

My wife, Ivy, and I were attending her friend's wedding in Tagaytay, a tony resort town south of Manila. The Swiss-styled resort, surrounded by fog-shrouded mountains, exuded the essence of a different time and place. But the wedding ceremony was pure Filipino, and therein lay its charm.

The dress code was specific: for principal sponsors like us, black coats or barongs for the men and long golden gowns for the women. For everyone else, strictly formal attire. That applied to the best man, maid of honor, groomsmen, bridesmaids, and all the secondary sponsors responsible, respectively, for the veil, the candles, and the cord. Add to that the bible bearer, ring bearer, coin bearer, flower girls and hordes of guests and you can begin to appreciate the lavish and utterly unique parameters of a Filipino wedding.

It is both charming *and* intimidating. Intimidating due to the abundance of black ties and the fact that you may be called upon at any moment—as I was—to offer an impromptu speech. Charming because it's all so formal, loving, and, well, *traditional.* Which is to say, *serious.*

Where I come from—specifically the wilds of Southern California—weddings, to the extent that they still happen at all, are taken with a grain of salt. That's because, statistically, nearly half of them aren't likely to last. And because most of the guests have probably already been divorced at least once or twice.

In the Philippines it's different. This is the world's last country—at least as of this writing—outside the Vatican that disallows divorce. So, when you get married in the Philippines, well, you'd better take it seriously.

In the real world, of course, Filipino couples separate all the time. And it can be reasonably argued—and frequently is—that the lack of legal divorce here forces people, especially women, to remain trapped in unhappy and unhealthy relationships. And yet, as I have previously written, there is something grudgingly admirable about a country that holds fast to the values of matrimony. That refuses to make it easy for families to unravel and disperse.

Since marrying one, I have sensed a real difference in the Filipinas I've encountered compared to their western counterparts. Though Filipino culture encourages and rewards feminine strength, it also embraces traditional values in matters of marriage and family. These women, though strong, still inhabit a universe in which men occupy an important and unambiguous place.

Which differs considerably from what I and scores of other Western men have experienced in post-feminist America. And so, part of me rejoices upon hearing matrimonial vows that take seriously the “bonds” of marriage. Or smiles at a ceremony celebrating Holy union as a forever commitment instead of merely one that’s convenient.

Which is why seeing a bride dance with her father almost brought me to tears. And why watching someone carry the cord to “bind us as one” inspires my inner cheers.

TURBULENCE

Everyone knows that airplanes crash.

That's why, for years, I've always contemplated death whenever boarding one. Could this, I can't help wondering, be when it happens? Am I taking my last trip?

Strangely, I forgot about all that recently while boarding a Cebu Pacific flight from Cebu to Surigao City. It was only a short domestic jump. And having just deplaned after a quick hop from Bacolod where we'd been partying with friends, well, sudden, horrific, agonizing death was the last thing on my mind.

Until we started landing at Surigao Airport.

Without warning, the plane began to rattle. Only slightly at first, but as we descended toward the runway, the rattle became a shake that turned into a roar. It was as if a giant hand had grabbed our craft and was waving it in the wind like a toy.

"Oh my God," Ivy said, "this doesn't feel right."

All around us, passengers sat in stunned silence as the walls of the airplane felt ready to crumble. Then, within a few feet of the ground, our plane suddenly pulled up. "So sorry," the captain calmly explained over the intercom. "We just made a missed approach because of high winds. We assure you that everything is under control; please bear with us while we try again."

That's when I started praying. "Please God," I silently repeated, thinking of the little ones waiting for us on the ground as we once again descended into the gust. "Don't let this happen to our children."

This time we got even closer before the captain, no longer able to tolerate the increasingly mad shudder, finally gave up. "I'm sorry," he repeated over the intercom, less calm than before. "We are proceeding back to Mactan."

And so we arrived in Surigao the next morning on the overnight ferry instead of by plane.

It wasn't the first time I'd encountered difficulties at Surigao Airport. Several years ago, in fact, I got ushered off a Manila-bound flight due to "mechanical issues." After a two-hour wait, the passengers re-boarded to hear an announcement. "Attention," the static-infested voice from the cockpit said before launching into an old familiar riff, "there's good news and bad." The bad news was that the airplane couldn't turn right. The good news: that there were no right turns en route to Manila.

Our local airport has certainly had its share of woes over the years. Back in 2017, a full 700 meters of the original 1,700-meter runway got destroyed by an exceedingly powerful earthquake. The damage led to the suspension of seven weekly Philippine Airlines flights between Manila and Surigao. By 2019, 400 of the wrecked meters had been restored. The remaining 300, I gather, are still somewhere in never-never land. Then, in 2021, the airport closed for 10 days because of the damage caused by Typhoon Odette.

Our wobbly would-be landing, of course, could have been much worse. Last year, 12 people got injured—some of them seriously—when a Qatar Airways flight from Doha to Ireland hit a bad patch of turbulence. About the same time, one passenger actually died and 100 others sustained injuries aboard a Singapore Airlines flight that rose 400 feet and then fell the same distance within a minute. And a recent *Washington Post* story reported on a United Airlines flight that took off from

Maui airport in Hawaii, ascended 2,200 feet into the sky and then, for reasons unknown, plunged 1,400 feet in 18 seconds, almost crashing into the sea.

Rod Williams, a 35-year-old real estate agent from Ohio, "looked across his two children to his wife," the newspaper reported, "both understanding the severity of the danger. They were scared. He started praying for God to send angels to help the pilots fly and land the plane safely. Then 'an unusual peace' came over him. 'You kind of have to accept that,' he said, 'because there's nothing you can do to change what's going on.'"

I too felt that peace. They say there are no atheists in crashing airplanes.

GROUNDED

I probably wouldn't have seen the film without first noticing the headline.

"Why is the movie *Plane* banned in the Philippines?" it asked, posing a provocative question indeed. Of course, I had to find out. So I hunted the darn thing down, finally finding it on Amazon Prime.

"It's movie night," I announced to my sweet wife who, it must be said, loves watching flicks as much as I do. And so we hunkered down.

An American action film starring Gerard Butler, the movie opened in US theaters on January 13, 2023. It would have been shown in the Philippines too, but for a move by the country's Movie and Television Review and Classification Board. Caving into demands by a vocal senator, the board pressured the movie's distributor into pulling it from Philippine theaters. Why? Because, according to its critic, "The reputation of our Motherland is at stake."

I understood his concern. The film depicts a commercial pilot—played by Butler—who, during a routine flight from Singapore to Honolulu, is forced by bad weather to land on the remote Philippine island of Jolo, in the Sulu Sea. "This island," the Filipino copilot warns, "is terrible. It's run by separatists and criminals. There's no government or police. If this is where we landed, we're not safe."

Indeed, within hours, the passengers—minus the pilot—are met by a gang of rebels who, after lopping off a head or two, take them all hostage. Which forces Butler and a cohort to embark on a dangerous mission to rescue them and save the day.

To be fair, the depiction is not without some basis in historical fact. Jolo, after all, served for many years as the jungle headquarters of Abu Sayyaf, the Philippines' most feared Islamic terrorist group. The same bunch that, in 2001, kidnapped American missionaries Martin and Gracia Burnham—briefly mentioned in the film—along with dozens of other captives, some of whom ended up dead. And it's the only place, during my brief stay in nearby Zamboanga two years later, that virtually everyone warned me against visiting.

Starting around 2017, however, the government says things improved. The number of terrorist attacks decreased dramatically. And some former rebel fighters are even reportedly being trained as guides to service an expected surge of tourists. So it's not surprising that politicians would want to avoid projecting negative images, but is banning movies the best way to go?

At least one group—the Directors Guild of the Philippines—thinks not. "To outright ban the film," the organization said in a statement, "is a cure much worse than the disease itself."

Most Filipinos seem to agree, judging from their reactions online. "...banning films on account of what is perceived as unfavorable to the Philippines," one declared in the *Philippine Star*, "is simply censorship...there will be no more freedom of expression."

A soon-to-be foreign immigrant to the country named Scotty agreed. "It is a fictional movie," he said, "but banning it will prove that it has some truth to it."

The one certainty is that everyone's now talking about a film that probably would have remained obscure. The probable outcome: lots more people will see it than ever would have before.

You can trust me on that because I'm one of them.

LOSING A CRANKY OLD FRIEND

A whack on the head.

That describes my first encounter with a jeepney. It happened 20 years ago during an early visit to Manila. I don't remember where I was headed or why, but my travel companion suggested we grab a jeepney.

And that's when it attacked me as I climbed aboard. "Ouch!" I howled, rubbing the bump on my forehead where the low-hanging ceiling had proffered a punch. "I don't think this vehicle likes Americans."

It was true; the jalopy-of-a-bus was clearly built for people half my size. Which was odd, given the ubiquitous mode of transportation's deep roots in its home country's long and complicated relationship with, you guessed it, the United States of America.

It all started after World War II when the departing US military gifted a man named Lamberto Tabing with an old Willys Jeep in gratitude for his services as a mechanic. Displaying traditional Filipino ingenuity, Lamberto added a roof and extended the vehicle's chassis, creating more seats to accommodate passengers. And, *voila!,* say hello to what's become—along with tricycles—the Philippines' most visible and iconic mode of public transportation.

Ah, but now its days may be numbered.

In Manila again last week, I noticed an angry-looking mob waving signs and hurling chants on a busy street. "It's the jeepney drivers," my non-jeepney Grab driver cheerfully explained. "They're on strike because the government is trying to force them out of business."

In fact, Malacañang's original proposal—put forward by former President Rodrigo Duterte and embraced by current President Ferdinand Marcos Jr.—would have phased out jeepneys as we know them by the end of 2023. Instead, drivers would be required to purchase more expensive modern minibuses with funds borrowed from government banks. The desired outcome: less congestion and pollution with more safety and comfort.

But drivers were less than enthusiastic regarding the plan. "To own a jeepney is like owning a caribou," Vince Tabing, the original inventor's grandson, told the *New York Times*. "A driver depends on it for a livelihood, much like a farmer depends on the beast."

To register their opposition, the jeepney driver/owners mounted a strike that was supposed to have lasted all week. On the third day, however, they voluntarily suspended it after Marcos promised to review the government's plans. The drivers "have made their point very clearly," the president told reporters in Quezon City.

As for me, well, I've strenuously avoided jeepneys anyway, ever since that first one smacked me on the noggin. And yet, the sight of these strange vehicles crowding the streets of Philippine cities has become synonymous with the country's culture.

The jeep-like bus "is now considered a cultural icon," Tabing told the newspaper. "It's a testament to [Filipino] ingenuity and innovation, making something beautiful out of an old engine and scrap metal."

I can't help but agree. Despite their general crankiness and hostility towards oversized foreigners, I would doubtless miss seeing those weird crawlers slowing traffic and blocking my way.

Let's just call it one of life's ironies in a country of confounding contrasts.

THE MEXICO OF ASIA

I still remember the first time I set foot in the Philippines. My immediate reaction was, "Wow, this is the Mexico of Asia."

That impression got reinforced last week during a seven-day sojourn to Mexico's seaside resort town of Mazatlán. "Wow," I heard myself thinking in a strange, reverse déjà vu, "this is the Philippines of North America."

It wasn't my first excursion to the United States' closest southern neighbor. Growing up in Southern California, in fact, I'd made many trips there as a rowdy young high schooler, mostly to the border town of Tijuana to taste the local tequila and flirt with wild bar girls willing to do almost anything for a couple of bucks.

I don't share this out of bravado, mind you, but to impart an idea of what life was like for a young gringo growing up near the border back in the crazy wrinkles of another time. Once my best friend, Ron, and I—feeling our oats and determined to lose our respective virginities—tried our luck at what we thought was a house of ill repute on one of the town's darkest corners. In the end, though, all we lost were the dollars in our pockets, confiscated by thugs dispatched to our rooms to shake us down.

"Geese, what just happened?" I asked my fellow would-be sinner, who I found sitting outside on a curb following our gut-wrenching ordeal.

"I'm not sure," Ron muttered.

Then we both broke into peals of laughter, finding humor where only demented teenagers would. Nothing to do, we figured, but continue south to Ensenada for our planned weekend of spearfishing, carousing and drunken debauchery.

As I matured, so did my Mexican journeys. In the mid-1970s, I spent a year studying creative writing at Instituto Allende, a small college just north of Mexico City, in a picturesque artist and writer's colony called San Miguel de Allende. "It's a quaint town with beautiful colonial-style buildings and cobblestone streets," I wrote years later. San Miguel, I continued, is "a birthplace of the Mexican revolution where patriots from throughout the country gather to pay homage to their history each year."

All that happened long before I ever laid eyes on the Philippines. And when I finally did, the strange sense of familiarity struck me like a liberated brick. The colors, smells, sounds—all bore Mexican flavors. My Filipino friends had Hispanic surnames. And lumbering along the highways with silver crucifixes dangling from their rearview mirrors, the discordantly colored jeepneys resembled Mexican buses.

The reason for these parallels is obvious: both countries spent centuries under Spanish rule. Hence, the architecture, religion, and customs all stem from common origins. And though each culture has since developed in its own uniquely delightful way, there is still a great deal they share.

"Beyond our historic ties," columnist Gideon Lasco has written in the *Philippine Daily Inquirer*, "contemporary Mexico can teach us so much about various issues [serving] as a mirror of our own experiences."

The recent journey to Mazatlán, ironically, transpired in the company of none other than my old friend, Ron, the same guy who, 55 years ago, sat laughing with me on a curb in Tijuana. Today we are both senior citizens, retired or semi-retired professionals, husbands, and grandfathers; far cries from what we were sitting on that fateful curb so long ago. Which explains why our most recent Mexican experience constituted a marked departure from those of the past; instead of lurking in dark rooms, we slept on comfortable beds, ate good food and relaxed with our oh-so-patient wives.

Not unlike how I now spend my time in the Philippines. The more things change, I guess, the more they stay the same.

SPELLING NAMES

It came up again the other night.

We were at the Gateway Hotel for a family dinner when my three-year-old niece slid unceremoniously under the table. “Ika!” I implored, using the only name I knew. “Get off the floor!”

When her mother chimed in, the little girl knew it was serious. “Zhiamae!” my sister-in-law sternly intoned. “Listen to your uncle!”

Wait, what did she say? More to the point, how the heck is it spelled? Oh yes, I recalled, it’s the name I can never remember. Welcome to the Philippines, where naming babies is a mysterious art and nicknames considered essential.

Here’s another barely recognizable name: Zhiamae’s older brother’s, Jacob. Simple enough, you’re probably thinking, what’s the problem? Just that it’s spelled J-h-a-i-c-o-b, which no one can ever pronounce or remember.

More strange Filipino names include Elijah spelled *Alijah*; Elgin as *Aelgenne*; Bartel as *Barthel*; and Jessica as *Jeasica*. And as if all that weren’t confusing enough, how about *Hazzel, Kristine, Wyndy*, and *Zhion* for Hazel, Christine, Wendy, and Zion? Oh, and let’s not forget our good friend Hershey, spelled *Her-she*.

I swear, it’s enough to make one’s head spin, specifically mine.

Apparently there's a reason for this ringing lack of rhyme. Anyone aware of Philippine history knows that it was long occupied and heavily influenced by a bevy of other nations, including Spain and, more recently, the US. So it's not too surprising that the country's native language is a hodgepodge.

Before the Spaniards arrived in the 16th century, the ancient *Tagalogs*—for whom the country' most widely spoken language is named—used the *baybayin* script in which to write. Later, it almost disappeared as the Spanish colonialists introduced the Roman alphabet. So, Tagalog and most other Philippine languages were written in *abecedario*, which was missing several letters. Then, in 1930, Filipino scholars introduced *abakada* comprising only twenty letters, including five vowels and 15 consonants. It was adopted as the official alphabet in 1941 although, according to at least one source, spelling was not completely standardized until the mid-20th century. Instead, she says, how one spelled depended on "the writer's preference."

But the confusing changes continued. Eleven letters were added in 1977 and, as recently as a decade later, several old ones were removed. Add to that the myriad of regional dialects and the emergence of English as a second national language and, well, it's certainly not shocking that the nation's spelling is confused.

It was amid this historical backdrop that we gathered at the Gateway Hotel for that recent evening of communal enjoyment. As I nibbled my chicken adobo and crunched the most amazing *Halo Halo* I'd ever tasted, I couldn't help but reflect on the evolution of this newly reborn country. Filipinos my age make up what can only be described as the nation's first post-colonial generation. And the hybrid culture they and their descendants forge will truly be a thing to behold.

One of those descendants—a teacher from Siargao Island named Jason—sat near me at the table. "Hey Jason," I called out, trying to be friendly, “come closer and don’t be so shy.” In the wide-ranging conversation that followed, he struck me as a reasonable and intelligent young man. Then I learned that he spells his name, *Gayson*.

Would someone please pass me a drink? A stiff one, if you don’t mind?

BOXER SHORTS

I meant it as a joke.

Back in 2019, I wrote a column called “Pajamas” aimed at a specific sort of reader; one completely comfortable with a narrator whose tongue was firmly planted in his cheek.

Subsequent events, however, have made me question my judgment.

That column was inspired by something I’d observed regarding a household employee during our early days in the Philippines, specifically, that the young woman insisted on working in her pajamas.

At first I thought I was mistaken. It was still early, I told myself. She had just prepared our breakfast and not had time to change. But, as the day wore on and she continued performing her duties without the benefit of street clothes or, dare I suggest, the services of a toothbrush, well, I realized that my thinking might just have to change.

Could the culture really be so different, I wondered, in this unfamiliar country to which I’d immigrated with nary a thought regarding what I should wear? Was this daytime pajama-wearing routine truly a national phenomenon, or just a millennial thing? And God forbid it was millennial, had the global culture already evolved beyond my grasp while I was looking the other way?

I later concluded with some confidence that indeed it had. The basis for that conclusion was a report regarding one of the judges at a recent Miss Philippines beauty pageant who showed up in his boxer shorts. "I chose to wear something made by a Pinoy," insisted Cecilio Asuncion, founder of a US-based transgender modeling agency whose ensemble also included a traditional barong along with leather boots and knee-high socks. "I love my country."

The story was reported on a website called *Coconuts Manila* under a headline spouting Asuncion's purported claim that his unusual attire represented "Filipino culture."

My reaction: finally, there's the proof!

Then I saw something else that further refined my understanding of the new world we all inhabit. They were images of an event that occurred in 2016 but hadn't reached my gaze until now; photos of fashion models walking down the runway at that year's Spring Fashion Week in Paris, France. Except the models weren't walking alone. Each strutted under the weight of another model "worn" as an accessory, usually positioned very oddly with butt up and head down.

The extra models were "human knapsacks" illustrating "the burden of life," audience members explained in social media posts regarding designer Rick Owens' avant-garde show. "The baggage we all carry is... each other."

The *Huffington Post*, dutifully reporting all this, even adding a quip of its own. The strange runway spectacles, the paper suggested, "give new meaning to [the idea of] women supporting one another."

And that's when the lightbulb flashed on in my head. Wearing pajamas or boxer shorts in public, I realized, is not a sign of laziness or a strange cultural affectation, but a fashion statement uniquely Filipino. Oh my God, I thought, how utterly sophisticated.

Then I read some of the social media reactions to Asuncion's culturally significant underwear. "Looks like sir forgot to wear pants," one observer wryly noted. Kind of like the emperor has no clothes.

Damn, I thought, back to the drawing boards I go.

HEY JOE

It happened again the other day.

I was riding my motorcycle along the coast towards downtown Surigao City, minding my own business, when a young boy by the side of the road let out a big whoop.

"Hey Joe!" he shouted with a huge grin and energetic wave.

And just like that, I was back at the start. More specifically, the start of my journey in this foreign land that now feels like home. In fact, I hadn't been called "Joe" in quite some time. But as any foreign white man in the Philippines will tell you, it's something we foreign white men get called a lot.

Occasionally, the moniker is uttered derisively with a smirk as if to say, "Hey, you foreign so-and-so, your presence is a stain." More often, though, it's meant as a friendly greeting, something akin to "Hey foreign guy, I see that you're white but don't worry because that's ok; in fact, I like it."

What's obvious, though, is that precious few of these self-appointed greeters—especially the kids—even know what they're saying.

Not that it's particularly poignant. The term originated in the aftermath of World War II when the Philippines was occupied by thousands of American "G.I. Joes" seen by many as their country's saviors.

The term actually started as the name of a 1941 cartoon character created by a US Army private named David Breger. Originally published in the *Saturday Evening Post* under the title "Private Breger," the strip quickly got snatched up and renamed by the Army.

To make a long story short, the term caught on and survives to this day as a popular line of action figures. For most Filipinos, though, it simply refers to any white man who looks like a foreigner. Which is to say, any white man they see.

I honestly don't know why, but after having it hurled at me regularly early on, it comes streaking in my direction far less often today. Is that because the designation has finally reached the early throes of a well-deserved and overdue death? Or because, having become a permanent resident, I'm now a familiar figure with a name of my own?

Either way, I can say with certainty that "Hey, Joe" is a greeting I do not crave.

Apparently others agree. Bob Martin, the American *Mindanao Bob* who once managed a website called "Live in the Philippines," said he "bristled every time I heard this being yelled at me, which meant three or four times every day..."

And Nathan Allen, a well-known American blogger who spent several years in the Philippines, expressed his sympathy for white non-Americans routinely assaulted by what many perceived as an unintended insult. "Personally," he wrote, "I don't mind it... but then again, I'm from the US. If I was British, German, or Russian, honestly, I might take offense..."

Ah, but then in 2020 America held an election that infused the designation with new dignity. "Well, what do you know?" columnist Mel Libre gushed in the *Sun Star*. "The 48th President of the United States is Joe Biden, and I don't think he'd mind if we'd greet him with the expression, 'Hey Joe!'."

Being less enamored of President Biden than is Libre, well, let me just say thanks, but no thanks.

My old mentor, Martin, however, came up with an ingenious solution. "I started using the term myself!" he wrote. "One day a friend and I were driving down the street, and we saw a foreigner... [So] I rolled down the window and yelled... 'Hey Joe!' The guy looked at me and you could see the shock on his face..."

So, fellow white guys, the next time you see me, just call me Joe. I'm kidding. Call me for a drink instead.

CRUELLY TORTURED (AMERICAN) PIGS

I suppose it was just a matter of time.

The day I first heard the anguished squeals of a terrified pig being slaughtered in the backyard of my then-fiancé's provincial Philippine home, my reaction was typically American: Oh my God, I thought, Muslim terrorists are cutting off heads!

Later, I witnessed the actual source of those squeals. It's difficult to explain the impact of such a sight on the tender psyche of someone for whom it is new. Difficult to explain, that is, to those who literally spend their lives within earshot of the final death squeals of cruelly tortured pigs. For a delicate soul like mine, the experience is akin to waking up, as a character in The Godfather once did, with a bloody severed horse's head next to him in bed.

Years of living in Mindanao eventually tempered that reaction. I became accustomed to the not-uncommon sight of crisp, full-bodied pigs laid out on tables as traditional Filipino *lechon*. The only thing missing was the apple in its mouth.

Ah, but now that typical Western reaction may be changing; cruelly tortured pigs, it seems, are coming to America. That, according to an article describing the first-ever Modern Homesteading Conference attended by 4500 Americans last month in Coeur d'Alene, Idaho. "At a time when obesity in the

US is at an all-time high," Olivia Reingold reported in *The Free Press*, "these homesteaders are bucking the convenience of cheap processed foods to grow their own produce in their backyards."

The best-attended demonstration at the two-day event: the do-it-yourself skinning and scalding of a whole pig destined for the dinner table. "A trailer yanks a hog carcass out of a bath of scalding water," the article reports. "Yellowjackets swarm the swine, now hanging by its hooves from the raised shovel of a trailer, as a man dressed in rubber overalls reaches for his knife."

Holy moly, is this really happening? And in America, no less? My God, will wonders never cease?

If this sort of thing catches on in the country of my birth, of course, millions of Americans will have to undergo the same radical attitudinal adjustment I experienced years ago in the Philippines. For me, it culminated on my 70th birthday, which began with the gut-wrenching squeals of a doomed little piggy being carried in a sack up our driveway to its slaughter. Try as I might, I couldn't resist following the jiggling bag all the way to the backyard where, as I watched fascinated, two neighbors unceremoniously dumped its contents onto an elevated board upon which the unfortunate animal's screeching throat was, even less ceremoniously, slit with a large gleaming knife. There was blood flowing every which way.

And that's when I noticed my remarkable calm.

It wasn't exactly the calm that emanates from deep within, the kind that finds its strength in a firm belief that the universe is good and all things ultimately stem from some divine and everlasting core. No, this calm merely said, "this too shall pass, and you shall survive." Unlike, I might add, that miserable pig. The calm that whispers a somewhat comforting message to the effect, more-or-less, that everything happens for a reason and it's all part of life's flow.

Here's the main takeaway; that there's actually some truth to our platitudes regarding life on this planet, specifically that living things are born and then they die. Pigs just do it sooner and more hideously. And too, one might conclude, their lives—unlike ours—almost invariably serve an immediate and obvious purpose.

Now, if only my fellow Americans can get all that...

RENEWAL

We'd been stalled in traffic for more than three hours when we finally called it quits. "Hey," I gingerly suggested to my publicist and driver, "I think it's time to stop."

I'd come to Manila to accomplish two things. First, the renewal of my Alien Certificate of Registration card bearing the 13A permanent resident visa that must be updated every five years. And second, as I would be there anyway, to do readings at Lyceum of the Philippines University in Intramuros, and at a high school in another part of town.

Lyceum had gone well, attracting a good-sized crowd with lots of questions regarding a foreigner's perceptions of the Philippines. Now we were en route to the high school, where my appearance was scheduled for 10 a.m. At 11:30, we were still seven kilometers away and standing still.

"I'm worried about getting to immigration in time," I said. "At this rate, we won't make it until well after closing!"

Patrick had to agree. And so, he placed the morning's umpteenth call, finally telling our hosts that we wouldn't be able to make it. "Manila traffic," he averred, a common excuse here requiring no further explanation. He reset the GPS, and 90 minutes later parked the car a few dozen blocks from the national Bureau of Immigration.

I felt confident, having carefully prepared all the documents mentioned during a similar visit months before. Ah, but then came the first of several snags; where, an immigration official wanted to know, was my barangay certificate of residency?

"Excuse me?" I said. "My what?"

"You need a statement from the barangay saying you live there," she explained.

Slowly, my blood rose. My home barangay was in Northern Mindanao, more than a 1000 kilometers away. "You mean I need to go back?" I stammered in what must have sounded like a forlorn plea. She just smiled and waved me away.

And that's when we hit on a daring plan. Commandeering my cell phone, I called my sister-in-law back in Surigao City. "Eva," I implored, "can you help me with something?"

Amazingly, she did just that; scooting down to the barangay office to make the request, she emailed me a copy of the required certificate within the hour. And thank God, the sour-faced immigration official agreed to accept a printout without the original.

But there were still other barriers to achieving complete legal recognition. A fully accomplished application. A notarized statement, signed by me, attesting to my residence in Punta Bilar. A special Power of Attorney and signed copy of my passport, enabling Patrick to pick up the new ACR card after seven working days. And, last but not least, a cool-looking folder with clips in which to bind everything tight.

All of which we miraculously accomplished after a few hours of scurrying between the various printers, copiers, legal offices, notaries, and stationery shops within easy walking distance.

Then came the *coup de grâce*: a 240 peso-per-month fine for not reporting the change of address that, according to my barangay certificate, had occurred in, hmmm, 2018? Which, of course, no one at the local immigration office in Surigao had bothered mentioning when I'd inquired about it several years earlier.

Still, we plowed on, finishing at 4:56 p.m. just four minutes before closing. We had no choice, given the card's scheduled expiration just two weeks hence. The final price tag: 17,000 pesos (around $300 US) in fines, fees, supplies, and professional services. Not to mention the even higher cost of a round-trip ticket to Manila and three nights in a local hotel.

But now I'm worried about how long it will take to get that darn new card. Seven business days doesn't seem like much, but there've already been two working holidays since I submitted my papers, with two more scheduled next week. As I've said many times, it's a manana culture.

The reassuring part of that culture, of course, is that even if we miss the deadline, they'll probably never get around to deporting me.

WHITE PRIVILEGE

It was an easy experiment with predictable results.

First my Filipino sister-in-law entered the mall. As always, the unsmiling security guard looked her over, asked her to open her purse, and explored its innards with a stick. Then nodded gruffly for her to pass.

Now it was my turn. Stepping up, I offered my bag for an equally thorough search. But the guard just smiled and waved me in. After which, my wife's sister and I looked at each other with amusement before dissolving into peals of unrestrained laughter.

White privilege.

Back in the USA, it's the object of piercing accusation and vociferous denial. Social justice warriors routinely call it out to shame those perceived as its beneficiaries. While more conservative folk like me, acknowledging the sometimes-significant role of white entitlement in the nation's history, argue that its effects are now largely mitigated by modern customs, sensibilities, and laws.

Things are noticeably different in the Philippines.

Here the contrasting deportment towards white foreigners and darker-hued natives is obvious to all. And yet it is viewed with amusement more often than rancor. And from the foreigner's point of view, it's as much a curse as it is a blessing.

There are several good things about being white in the Philippines. Almost everyone calls you sir. No one complains if you cut in line. And, as previously noted, you can sometimes enter malls without opening your bag for inspection.

The list of negatives for foreigners of *any* hue, however, is far more substantial. You can't own land, are barred from taking part in politics or protests, and are often expected to pick up the dinner tab for everyone with whom you dine.

Bottom line: the Filipino relationship to foreigners, especially white ones, is complicated. I don't pretend to understand it. What I suspect, though, is that it has a great deal to do with economics, colonialism, and war.

Race relations in America are steeped in history, too. The United States, after all, allowed slavery until the mid-19th century, fought a ferocious civil war to end it, and endured a long civil rights movement to ensure equal liberties for all. And yet, ironically, Americans seem more obsessed with race today than ever before.

During much of my life, for instance, certain racial minorities have benefited from special consideration in college admissions and hiring through a government-enforced policy called affirmative action. Last year the US Supreme court wisely banned race-based preferences in education after Asian Americans—including Filipinos—deemed it unfair. And now my home state of California is considering legislation to gut that decision by allowing governor-granted "exceptions" to the non-discrimination rule.

"Will they ever give up?" columnist William McGurn wondered in a recent *Wall Street Journal* piece entitled *Making Discrimination OK Again*. "Those looking to divvy up Americans by race, that is."

Here in the Philippines it's less black and white, to use a well-worn pun. Though racial differences are obvious and openly acknowledged, they don't seem to be a source of major conflict. Sometimes humor intervenes, as in the comical comparisons of the popular skin-lightening products here vs.

the fly-off-the-shelves sun-tanning lotions on foreign shores. And, like anywhere, ethnic and racial differences disappear as social intercourse and friendships grow.

I was still in junior high school when legendary civil rights guru Martin Luther King delivered his most famous speech. "I have a dream!" he bellowed to a crowd of 250,000 gathered at Washington D.C.'s Lincoln Memorial. "I have a dream that my four little children will one day live in a nation where they will be judged not by the color of their skin but by the content of their character."

Words to live by. Perhaps even more now than on the momentous day they were uttered.

COMMUNE OR CULT?

We were a mile off the coast of a remote Philippine island when I realized the boat was sinking.

The island in question was Bucas Grande, off the Northern Mindanao coast. Eventually, a sympathetic octopus fisherman, noting our panicked bailing, gave us a tow. And that was the first time, some 20 years ago, that I ever set foot in Socorro, a charming little coastal town recently infamous for reasons you might know.

Back then, the town's most notable feature was a luscious fountain I later learned had ostensibly sparked the famous "Colorum" uprising of 1924. Billed in America as a bloody rebellion by religious fanatics, it resulted in hundreds of deaths and the ruthless torching of the town. By the time I visited the dissidents' hilltop compound a century later, however, the violence had simmered down.

You can imagine my excitement, therefore, upon hearing that yet another strange and ominous "doomsday cult" had sprung up in Socorro. This one, known officially as Socorro Bayanihan Services Inc., comprises about 3,500 members inhabiting a 355-hectare mountain enclave called Kapihan. And just last month, several of its members—including leader Jey Rence Quilario, a.k.a. Senor Aguila—got arrested for serious crimes.

"This is a harrowing story of rape, sexual violence, child abuse, [and] forced marriage perpetrated on minors by a cult,"

Senator Risa Hontiveros told the Senate. “This cult is armed and dangerous.”

So, naturally, I had to go say hello.

The trip from Surigao City is not arduous. It begins with a roughly two-hour drive down the coast to Hayanggabon Port in Claver, followed by an hour-long boat ride to Socorro. Our first stop was City Hall, where I met Edelito Sangco, municipal agriculturist and chairman of the Socorro Task Force Kapihan.

“I’m their public enemy number one,” he declared, adding that tourism in Socorro has dropped 62% because of fear induced by the widespread media coverage.

In Sangco’s telling, the problem began with drugs. Eventually, he said, it evolved into the believers’ view of Aguila as the reincarnated Child Jesus who would protect them from all harm. To avail themselves of that protection, some members allegedly sold their homes, quit their jobs, left their spouses, and forced their children into unwanted illegal marriages. At its height, Sangco said, the encampment was heavily guarded by armed members especially trained for the task.

“It’s dangerous for us to go there,” Sangco concluded, referring to himself and other accusers.

And so the city provided a police escort for me, my wife, and a Filipino friend. Riding in the back of an emergency vehicle driven by a uniformed officer, we scooted for about 25 minutes along winding mountain roads traversing beautiful lakes and streams.

These days the compound is guarded, not by residents, but by a squad of uniformed police. One of them, shouldering an M16 rifle, accompanied us on foot along a series of muddy paths connecting shabby tin-roofed houses.

“The charges are fabricated,” insisted Roharosenyll Dotillos, 54, a former teacher in Socorro who now helps manage Kapihan. “Here we live by the Bible as one family. The love, unity, and cooperation is real.”

Gilbert G. Dizon, a 39-year-old skilled laborer, said residing in Kapihan makes him feel safe.

And Patchulo Curambao, 40, said he came for the simple life. "The allegations," he said, "are all lies."

Yet former members in town swear they are true. "We've seen it for ourselves," declared one, who preferred to remain anonymous for fear of repercussions.

So who to believe?

I can honestly say I sensed no hostility or disingenuousness at Kapihan. At one point, a large group of smiling children spontaneously welcomed us with shouts and waves. And in a nearby gymnasium, a young drum-and-bugle core practiced military cadences before an adoring crowd.

Still, one can't dismiss the tears of those claiming to have been woefully wronged. My heartfelt conclusion? Let me just put it this way: thank God I'm not the judge.

ANXIETY

I was having dinner with a Filipino friend at a Manila restaurant recently when he pulled out a card. The check had just arrived, and I wondered whether he was offering to cover it.

"I've got a disability," he explained, "and it's worth a 20% discount!"

"Does it include me?" I jokingly wondered, making light of his pronouncement.

"It includes anyone I'm with," my friend declared.

"Wow," I said, genuinely interested now. "If you don't mind my asking, what's your disability?"

"Anxiety," he said, and just like that, my world was changed. "You can also get a discount for depression."

All of which was news to me. And which, I might add, plunged me into a state of deep introspection. Back home in the US, you can get a special parking permit if you live in a wheelchair, have no legs, or your arms are amputated above the elbows. Short of that, well, good luck in making it safely to the front entrance of your local mall.

Here in the Philippines, apparently, it's different.

My friend said he got his disability card after spending two months in the hospital last year for treatment of pneumonia and a collapsed lung. The experience was so stressful, he said, that he lapsed into a state of almost constant anxiety. So, he saw a psychologist who certified his ragged state of mind. Then applied for a disability identification card from the office of the Philippines National Council on Disability Affairs. Its mission:

to assure inclusive education, provide economic empowerment, harness technology and innovation, and oversee humanitarian concerns on behalf of disabled people.

Which is how he now rates a legally mandated 20% discount on almost anything he buys. Even though, to untrained eyes like mine, he seems no more anxious than the rest of us, including me.

"Wow!" I repeated, this time genuinely impressed, "I want to get me one of those cards!!"

There are genuine reasons, of course, why disability discounts for anxiety and depression aren't readily available in the United States. Perhaps the most obvious is that, if they were, practically everyone in America would be on disability.

But there's also another, even more pressing, motivation for keeping discounts out of the hands of anxious Americans: making those symptoms disappear is a booming business. "A search for 'anxiety relief' on Google pulls up links for supplements in the form of pills, patches, gummies, and mouth sprays," begins a *Wall Street Journal* article on the subject headlined 'The Booming Business of American Anxiety.' "There are vibrating devices that hang around your neck...weighted stuffed animals, bead-filled stress balls and coloring books that claim to bring calm."

Not to mention, of course, the scads of online therapists and "anxiety coaches" available to calm your nerves for a price.

"Americans are anxious," the newspaper concludes, "and a flurry of old-line companies, upstarts and opportunistic entrepreneurs aim to fill the demand for relief."

All of which is fine, I suppose, if you have the money to pay for it. But I don't. And, anyway, I live in the Philippines. Which leaves me with just one burning question: where do I sign up for my personalized anxiety discount card?

Not knowing is making me anxious.

WATER

I was lathered to the gills, about to step under the spigot, when the darned thing just choked up.

"Damnit!" I shouted, loud enough, I imagined, for passersby on the street below to hear the furious reverberations emanating from my shower stall. "What the hell am I supposed to do now?"

Water.

Its presence soothes and sustains. Its absence makes you insane. I've been feeling that way a lot lately. Perhaps I should try to explain.

There are two basic problems feeding the seemingly endless toilet, shower, and sink woes tormenting the Haldane household in Surigao City. The first is that we reside too far out of town to be connected to the municipal water line. So, every three weeks or so we have to pay someone to deliver a huge tanker full of H2O.

The bigger issue, though, is that our house sits atop a hill. Which requires us to pump that water up from a street-level tank. Welcome to the source of an eternal tug-of-war with the forces of science, nature, and technology that leaves us bone dry way too often and for far too long.

Ok, let me just say it right up front, something I've often thought but never had the temerity to utter out loud until now. I'm no plumber, but the one who designed this so-called water system was more insane than I feel standing naked and soapy in my shower.

Pipes and valves run everywhere. While some supposedly feed a second tank up high, others flow directly into our tri-level house. The annoying result: an almost constant game of musical pails in which each of our three floors competes with the others to trick us into utilizing showers that won't sprinkle and toilets that won't flush.

"OK, I give up!" I've hollered into the mirrors on more than one occasion. "You've snookered me again. Congratulations!!"

Sometimes the system works fine. Usually just long enough to loll us into a complacency that allows the pipes to regroup for another attack. Then we call the guy who acted as foreman during construction, the only human we know with even a modicum of understanding about how it all works.

Under his tutelage, we have purchased two new pumps and tanks, repositioned them repeatedly, and frequently stood by holding our breaths while he wiggled a valve or pushed on a pipe. Then exhaled just long enough to take a few showers before the water again disappeared.

This morning, though, I reached a whole new level of angst. Perhaps it was because I'd just returned from a week in primitive quarters on Siargao Island, where I'd become accustomed—as are many Filipinos—to dumping buckets of cold water over my head every day. Wow, I thought, caked with soap in the waterless shower stall upon my return, what I wouldn't give for a bucket right now.

That did it.

The day pouring frigid water over your head seems like a good idea is a day crying desperately for change. *Radical* change. The kind of change requiring bold new ideas. The sort of change that needs a new expert with major plumbing skills and an unprecedented plan.

We may have found someone fitting that bill. Just to be safe, though, we're also looking for a priest to bless our newly redesigned water system once it's installed. Maybe that's the only way to finally exorcise the nasty demons inhabiting our pipes.

In the meantime, please wish us luck as you picture me shivering sloppily in that godawful waterless shower. And, in case we don't find that priest, please pray that there will never be a shortage of buckets.

SPUTTERING SOLAR

If only the sputtering would stop.

It attacks suddenly, like an enemy soldier watching from a nearby bush. Everything is still for hours. Then, just as you're beginning to relax thinking your travails are over, out it jumps, spraying the landscape with the rat-a-tat-tat of eye-numbing darkness.

I'm talking about our recent conversion to solar energy at the hilltop house we built in Mindanao. It certainly seemed like a good idea at the time. Being from Southern California, we were familiar with the many benefits of solar. Aside from helping the environment, of course, it can be extremely helpful to your pocketbook.

So it wasn't hard saying yes several years ago when a man knocked on the door of our then-home in the only American state requiring solar photovoltaic systems in every newly constructed house. Because our house wasn't new, the stranger made us an offer we couldn't refuse.

"Tell you what," he said, or words to that effect. "My company will install, maintain, and operate solar panels on your roof if you commit to buying your electricity from us." Oh yes, he added, and "just to make it worth your while we'll give you $1,500."

That sealed the deal. And everything worked precisely as promised; though we still had to buy our electricity, it was considerably cheaper than we'd been paying the electric company for years.

Then we moved to the Philippines.

Let me begin by saying that, yes, we did build a fairly large house here. That said, let me also add that its electric bills have been staggeringly higher than we've ever paid anywhere, including California. And so we began searching for the soothing light of the sun.

We got two bids before deciding, one more than twice as high as the other. But even the lower price required my poor, hard-working Filipino wife to put in several extra months at her well-paying job abroad. Ah, but then she came home with the cash and the rest worked out like a dream.

I'm kidding, it's been more like a jerkily flickering nightmare. We'd be watching a movie when suddenly the power would go off. Or the bedroom air conditioner would start stuttering and have to be reset.

Then it got worse. Everything would shut down repeatedly, beginning around 7 p.m., then again at 5 in the morning. And the power would stay off until someone staggered into the basement to fiddle with an amorphous array of switches, one of which eventually did the trick. Or, sometimes, until realizing that none would do the trick at all.

Living in the provinces, of course, we'd grown accustomed to occasional brownouts. Which is why we own a diesel generator to bridge those horrible gaps. But going solar was supposed to fix all that; instead, the situation just kept getting worse.

Naturally, we constantly tormented the guy—a fellow expat—who'd sold us the thing and, to his credit, he'd dutifully show up. Acting on his instructions, we added an automatic voltage regulator, replaced several breakers, rewired the clothes dryer, and overhauled the new solar battery.

Nothing helped.

Finally, he brought in a bona fide Filipino electrician who replaced the automatic transfer switch with a bigger one and, voila!, our lights went right back on. Ok, that's an exaggeration; let's just say that we're back to flickers with only *occasional* full-scale brownouts.

Ah, but this morning we got some excellent news. Our application for net metering has been approved. So soon we'll be receiving credits from the local power utility for electricity we generate but don't use. Which means that, with any luck, our next electric bill should be low enough to touch the ground.

The only downside is living with the sputter.

CALICO CAT

It was just a cat.

Not unlike the many that wander into our house making themselves at home. Nobody seems to know who owns them. My guess is that they just live in the barangay, migrating to wherever they can find food and shelter. Oh yes, and a private corner in which to do their stinky business.

This particular cat, though, had a distinguishing feature: it was a Calico. That rare and gorgeous white-streaked-with-gold breed that some cultures worship as goddesses of love, beauty, and fertility. Almost invariably female, many see them as symbols of feminine power and grace. And nearly everyone believes they bring good luck and good fortune.

So I issued stern orders to everyone in the house: feed it, indulge it, but please never chase it away. Because, God knows, we need good fortune as much as the guy down the road.

I should probably explain that my orders must have seemed confusing. Because—ok, I'll confess it right here—I had taken our previous feline squatter on a long ride from which she never returned. Deeply annoyed at the animal's uncanny ability to find her way into the house even when we thought all its entrances were blocked, compounded by her propensity for jumping on the table to eat our dinner, well, I reached out one day and gave that cat a pat.

Almost immediately, she relaxed, clearly unaccustomed to this rare show of human affection.

Then I grabbed the animal by the scruff of its neck and dragged it, kicking, to the car. With an obedient niece holding the beast as far from her vitals as possible, I drove us all towards downtown. And about 10 kilometers later, pulled over and quickly threw open the door.

"Ok," I told my trembling young niece, "time to let that baby go!"

As we sped off, I got a last glimpse of the forlorn cat through the rear-view mirror, looking wildly hurt and confused as it disappeared behind a bush. My only defense is that it wasn't a Calico.

In fact, the real Calico might have escaped the same fate had it not made the fatal mistake of delivering kittens. Given its karma-enhancing powers, I was ready to let that go. But soon the kittens started disappearing, only to be traced days later by their small piles of four-smelling excrement left in otherwise forgotten corners. And, sure enough, the nieces charged with cleaning those hidden corners quickly complained.

Then one day I came home to the absence of our Calico. And yet, its more ordinary kittens were still roaming about. "Alright," I said, trying to suppress the surge of anger rising within me. "What happened to our cat?"

One of the nieces, probably the one who drew the shortest straw, bravely stepped forward. "Umm," she began. "Well..."

"Yes?" I demanded impatiently.

"We couldn't stand the smell," she finally admitted, "so we took her for a ride."

"And the kittens?" I pointedly inquired.

"We couldn't catch them," the young woman confessed. "We'll try again tomorrow."

So a house full of Calico had been reduced to one of nondescript kittens.

"Do you honestly think this is better?" I couldn't help but inquire. "Separating the kittens from their mother?"

She met my question with a shrug, so I grunted and marched up the stairs.

A few days later, the same niece met me at the stairway's bottom. "We got rid of those kittens," she announced, "at the same place we took their mom."

"How will they survive?" I inquired skeptically.

Then she delivered the punchline. "You won't believe this," she said, "but their mother was still sitting there waiting."

I *didn't* believe it. I figured they'd just made that up to placate my feelings. Happily, it worked. Less happily, however, I'm still looking over my shoulder for the crushing bad fortune sure to come.

CRUELLY TORTURED CATS

It looks like I've finally hit a nerve. By which I mean, written something brazenly offensive enough to inspire hate mail.

No, the offending column didn't reference the war in Gaza nor critically address life and governance in the Philippines.

In fact, what drew the wrath of more than a few readers was my blatant confession of an unforgivable sin: moving a misbehaving stray cat from one location to another.

"You're a jerk, David," began one of the 83 comments left on Facebook, where I'd posted my errant piece after it appeared in the newspaper. "Show affection to a poor cat, then...take it far away and throw it out of the car into an uncertain future? I stopped reading your drivel right then and there. I hope you see that cat's forlorn face in your last days."

Here's how another reader assessed my journalistic abilities: "An absolutely disgusting article that shows how arrogant some humans can be. You should just stop writing about topics you have no heart for...or simply retire. This was pure garbage."

At issue was my recent column entitled "Calico Cat." In it, I recalled the tale of a stray in our neighborhood that, despite our best efforts, continuously found its way into our house, jumped onto our table, and insisted on sharing our dinner even after we'd fed it leftovers. Eventually we solved the problem by transporting the delinquent feline several kilometers down the road, where—far from "throwing it out of the car"—we gently lowered it to the welcoming ground.

"Hmm, you think you will get away with this?" warned the same reader who'd urged my early retirement. "Just you wait. Karma has your name, and she's my friend."

Ok, I'll admit it, that one worried me just a bit.

At least one reader, though, offered what seemed like sensible advice. "The better option," she suggested, "should have been to trap, neuter/spay, and release."

As fate would have it, I spent last weekend on Siargao Island, where a medical mission was visiting my wife's hometown of Pilar. And, wouldn't you know it, one of the visiting missionaries was, yes, a veterinarian.

"Let's go see what they're doing," Ivy urged, and so we did.

The first thing I noticed was a small, locked cage containing an extremely nervous-looking cat. "What are you doing?" I inquired.

"Oh," the vet replied nonchalantly, "not much, just neutering." It was perfect, like a message straight from Karma herself. And so I made myself comfortable and sat down to watch.

The vet pulled out an exceedingly long needle. Then, grabbing an enormous chunk of the terrified cat's flesh, sank that steel in. Almost immediately, the animal went limp. But its eyes stayed wide open, still looking terrified as it tried to discern what was about to happen in its nether regions.

Next came the gleaming silver knife, shiny and sharp. The doctor unceremoniously spread open the animal's hind legs. And that's when I turned away, unable to watch any longer. I don't know how other men feel, but I get extremely uneasy at even the thought of a cutting tool anywhere near the area of my scrotum. And so I closed my eyes, trying to obliterate the disturbing images popping up behind their lids.

"Daddy," my 4-year-old daughter offered helpfully, "the cat has blood on it."

Oh great, I thought, thanks for the lovely picture. When it was all over, that poor cat—still dazed—lay panting on its side. But all I could see was the sheet underneath it, spattered in red.

OK, I'm probably gonna catch hell for saying this, but...well...if it were me, I think I'd rather just get banished to a new neighborhood.

5.
WAR

REST IN PEACE UNCLE JORGE

This is the story of a man and his hat.

The hat is a military green cap adorned at its front by a bright red star. The man is George Madlos, commander, activist, and spokesman for the National Operations Command of the New People's Army. Until recently, he was also the most wanted communist insurgent in the Philippines.

For many decades, the hat and man were inseparable as the former rode proudly on its owner's head, fomenting revolution in the jungles of Mindanao. Now they are forever parted; Madlos consumed by the cremationist's flames while the hat rests patiently on the mantel of a friend.

In fact, the parting occurred amicably several years ago, the last time Fernando Almeda saw the legendary rebel who had long been his compadre. "I urged him to give himself up," the noted historian told me recently, proffering the hat for my examination. "I argued that communism would never triumph here like it did in Cuba; that he would never be another Che Guevara."

Jorge's response, Almeda says, was quiet but firm.

"It's too late to change," he recalls the radical telling him. "He said he would die fighting for his cause."

Then the famous revolutionary handed Fernando his cap, just as Fernando would one day hand it to me. "Keep this as a memento," Madlos instructed. "Please display it in a museum when I am dead."

That day has now come. The soft-spoken rebel recently died of gunshot wounds after—depending on who you believe—engaging in a skirmish with the military in Bukidnon or getting ambushed by government soldiers while riding a motorcycle to his doctor's office.

"George Madlos' reign of terror has finally ended," Army commander Major General Romeo S. Brawner Jr. declared afterwards. "Now, justice has been served for those innocent civilians and their communities that he terrorized for several decades."

There's a joke on Siargao Island, where both Madlos and my wife were born, that people from there should never marry each other because they're probably related. As news of the legendary guerilla's death spread like wildfire throughout his home province of Surigao del Norte last week, I couldn't help but believe that to be true: the outlaw revolutionary was the uncle of one of our best friends on the island and distantly related to my wife's own cousin.

But there's another reason I feel connected to him, and it's related to history. Madlos was exactly my age, so it's a good bet that his radicalization as a young man in Mindanao occurred about the same time mine happened in New York City. I joined a Marxist group called the Young Socialist Alliance to work as a political organizer. And, though I never took part in revolutionary violence or got arrested like Madlos, I certainly believed in the overthrow of global capitalism.

Before too long, though, I figured out that our planned Marxist revolution—assuming we could pull it off—would mark not only a personal disaster but a historic catastrophe. Replacing capitalism with any Marxist-inspired alternative, I realized, was not only unrealistic, but exceedingly dangerous based on the examples provided by virtually every place in the world it's been tried. So how, I wonder now, does a presumably intelligent man like Madlos commit himself exclusively to such an idea and follow it all the way to his grave?

Surviving family members unanimously describe the man as considerate, gentle, loving, and kind, despite multiple criminal charges against him involving murder, robbery, and damage to property. Madlos' nephew recently posted a tribute beginning with the words "Rest in peace Uncle Jorge." A niece, now living in America, penned several posts, describing the hand-painted birthday cards, wedding congratulations, and life-affirming advice he offered over the years in clandestine meetings hidden from the eyes of those who would eventually kill him.

"To the world you are a bad person," she wrote. "To me and the rest of the family, you are simply the soft-spoken uncle. People may think that you speak with a booming voice [but] yours was the softest voice yet filled with conviction."

I may never understand how someone like George Madlos arrives at that kind of conviction, rationalizes it, and makes it the core of his existence. In an eight-year-old video that's one of the most touching I've ever seen, Uncle Jorge himself attributes the strength of his beliefs to "my silent revolutionary mother." Whatever one thinks of those notions and the actions they inspired, for me the main takeaway is this: that the world's perceptions seldom reflect the complete dimensions of a man's soul.

And what of his long-suffering hat?

Almeda says he will eventually place it in a museum of Surigaonon heritage now under construction in Surigao City. Once that happens, I suppose, I'll be making lots of pilgrimages there to gaze upon that iconic symbol of revolution. And contemplate the powerful ironies embodied in its presence.

STANDING IN

I had an entirely different lead in mind for this piece.

I expected it to say that the annual Battle of Surigao Strait commemoration took place last week, but with a minor difference; instead of viewing it from the stands as usual, I viewed it from my house across the street.

Then came a knock on the door.

Major Eric Richards, Ground Programs Chief for the Joint US Military Assistance Group at the US Embassy in Manila, couldn't make it, a pleasant young woman informed me. Would I, she wanted to know, be willing to stand in for him to represent my country? The rehearsal, she said, was 4 p.m. followed by the ceremony at 6 the next morning.

And that's how it came to pass that, instead of relaxing in my underwear over coffee, I spent the morning standing at black-tie attention next to the mayor of Surigao City.

Perhaps a little background is in order.

I'd been involved in the yearly remembrance of history's last major naval battle almost since arriving in the Philippines. That's mostly because my house overlooks the spot in Northern Mindanao where that conflict occurred; the deceptively placid piece of ocean in which America and its allies beat back the forces of Imperial Japan in 1944, paving the way for Gen. Douglas MacArthur's promised return.

It's also where, three years ago, the city dedicated its magnificent Battle of Surigao Strait Memorial and Museum to host annual remembrances of that historic event. So—being the closest neighbor and only American around—it wasn't too surprising that they asked me to join the memorial's oversight council, for which I'd attended the annual commemorations regularly as an observer, though not a participant.

But recent events altered the landscape, both literally and figuratively.

First, the pandemic put everything on a two-year hiatus. Then the horrific Typhoon Odette tore off the museum's roof, scattering its contents to the four winds. And, finally, a recent change in local leadership put the memorial's future in doubt.

Initially, word was that the new mayor considered it part of the old mayor's agenda, and thus unworthy of his support. But then, suddenly, like a bolt of lightning from heaven, a bulldozer showed up unannounced one day to make the needed repairs. And in a development both disheartening and encouraging, the mayor dissolved our oversight council to appoint a new task force all his own.

So it was with mixed emotions I prepared to watch this year's proceedings from my veranda across the street instead of in the stands. Then came the knock that changed all those plans.

"You're the only American we know," the young woman beseeched. "You'll probably be the only one there."

Thus, I couldn't say no.

It rained mightily on the morning of the event. Another young woman, bearing an enormous umbrella, met me at the memorial's entrance and showed me to my seat under the cupola of honor. Later I stood with a hand over my heart watching the American flag hoisted to the strains of the Star-Spangled Banner. And then—along with those representing the Philippines, Australia, and Japan—thrust a blazing torch forward to help light an eternal flame of remembrance.

At a welcoming dinner the night before, I'd sat with the new mayor and chatted. "What do you think of my administration so far?" he asked at one point.

"Well," I responded, somewhat at a loss for what else to say, "I certainly like what you're doing with the memorial."

In the end, my participation was rewarded with a majestic green ribbon adorned with golden beads, a lovely basket of exotic local delicacies, and an impressive wooden plaque in honor of "his invaluable presence."

I hardly even noticed that the name it bore wasn't mine.

TRAVELING DANGEROUSLY

The woman at the ticket counter looked like she'd seen a ghost.

"You want to go where?" she asked. "Zamboanga? Don't go there. The Muslim terrorists will cut off your head."

Not quite what I'd expected from a Philippine Airlines employee checking me in for my very first flight to the Philippines. "But I have to," I countered, rather meekly, I'm afraid. "I'm going to see a woman I met online and have already bought a ticket."

"Meet her in Manila!" the Filipino ticket taker almost commanded.

In the end, I didn't cancel my flight. Instead, I paced up and down the terminal corridor for an hour, trying to summon the courage to board that plane. Which was only accomplished, finally, with the help of tranquilizers and an alcoholic beverage or two. All that happened more than 20 years ago. Now, they tell me, military officials are calling for tourists to come on back and be guided by those selfsame terrorists.

"Sulu is relatively peaceful," Brig. Gen. Benjamin Batara has insisted, speaking of the island province just off the Zamboanga Peninsula in southern Mindanao. Previously, the area's chief claim to fame was as headquarters for Abu Sayyaf, the country's cruelest band of Islamic insurgents. But times have changed, according to the general. "For quite a long time, there's been an absence of violent clashes."

Batara was speaking at the ceremonial groundbreaking of a 25-million-peso reformatory then being built for former members of the radical Islamist group that terrorized southern Mindanao for more than three decades. When completed, he said, the halfway house will serve as a center for what the *Philippine Daily Inquirer* calls "ideological reorientations and livelihood training to help them integrate into mainstream society."

"There is a marked change in the peace and order," Batara said. "The last kidnapping was more than two years ago."

Indeed, there have been a few changes since my first flight to Zamboanga. In the last five years, authorities say, more than 400 Abu Sayyaf warriors have surrendered to the government. Recently Sulu, Basilan and Tawi-Tawi—all former terrorist strongholds—signed an "integrity pledge" ahead of the country's last general election. And in Basilan, the wives of former Moro Islamic Liberation Front fighters have started a program to keep toy guns away from their children.

"They are just toys," one mother explained, "but the way [they] have been ingrained in the minds of our young kids, there's a corresponding price to pay...Banning these toy guns...will encourage children to be better members of society."

All of which differs from the atmosphere prevailing in the area back in 2002. Landing at Zamboanga's airport that first time, we were literally escorted off the tarmac between lines of well-armed guards. I remember feeling almost imprisoned at the Garden Orchid Hotel where protective security guards, also armed with carbines, watched my every move. And when a Muslim police friend offered to set me up for an exclusive interview with an Abu Sayyaf fighter in Jolo, well, I felt compelled to turn him down. No point, I figured, in making myself available for a terrorist kidnapping.

Three years later, returning to the city on assignment for the *Los Angeles Times*, I had a somewhat different experience. For starters, the then-reigning Miss Zamboanga and provincial tourism director met me at the airport for a guided tour. And yet, one woman I interviewed lived in a house still punctured by bullet holes from a recent rebel attack.

But I'm glad to hear that things are finally settling down in southern Mindanao. That said, will I rush out tomorrow to buy a ticket for the country's newest tourist hotspot?

Let me put it this way: if you go first, I may follow.

FILIPINO LOVE

She could have been my sister-in-law.

Angelyn Aguirre, a 32-year-old native of Pangasinan, had spent the last six years working as a caregiver in Israel. This December, according to her family, she planned on returning to the Philippines permanently to raise a family with the man she married last year.

Instead, she flew home in a coffin after being brutally murdered by Hamas terrorists. Her sin: refusing to leave the side of her elderly employer, who the terrorists also killed. “Unimaginable honor in the face of evil,” Jerusalem Deputy Mayor Fleur Hassan-Nahoum said of Aquirre’s last moments. “Despite having a chance to flee, Angelyn showed unbelievable humanity and loyalty by remaining...”

She was one of four Filipinos killed in the horrific attacks of Oct. 7, 2023, during which more than 1200 Israelis were murdered and several hundred more taken hostage. As the subsequent clouds of war darkened Israeli skies, the Philippine government prepared to evacuate some of the estimated 30,000 Filipinos in Israel, especially those in the areas most likely affected. “The Philippines will always stand with Israel,” President Marcos is said to have assured Israeli Ambassador Ilan Fluss.

Which doesn’t surprise me at all.

In my five-plus years as a Jewish-American expat in the Philippines, I have often felt the full force of Filipino love. It is warm. It is encompassing. And it offers comfort as a soothing, solicitous, solace.

Filipinos actually have a longstanding special relationship with Jews. During the Holocaust, which claimed the lives of several of my forebears, the Philippines was one of the world's few countries offering haven to otherwise untethered European Jewry. In fact, there was—and remain some vestiges of—a fully functioning, vibrant, Jewish community in Manila that was at least 1200 strong.

"My father got a lot of positive attention," one refugee, who arrived at age eight, later wrote in a memoir recalling the experience. "There was an element of something so redemptive."

Lotte Hershfield, a German Jew whose family emigrated to the Philippines in 1938, later described the experience as life-altering. "We would not be alive today if not for the Philippines," she told CNN decades later. "We would've been destroyed in the crematorium."

A monument erected in 2009 at Israel's Holocaust Memorial Park in the shape of three open doors gives thanks to the Filipino people for saving so many Jewish lives. And to this day, Israel maintains special bilateral trade agreements with the Philippines for goods and services worth more than $530 million US annually. It also encourages its companies to invest in the country, provides disaster aid and military training, and allows Filipinos to enter Israel visa free.

It "was like a rebirth," documentary filmmaker Noel Izon has said of the Jewish experience in the Philippines during World War II. "They went from certain death to [the promise of] life."

Which, metaphorically, kind of describes what I've experienced in the Philippines as well. Though certainly never facing death in America, being in the Philippines has indeed afforded me a new life. It is where I am raising my children. And it is where I feel most at home.

I have spoken often of a Jewish religious obligation called "making *Aliya*," an obligatory return to the land of Israel before one dies. I have not yet done that. And yet, in some ways, I feel like the Philippines *is* my Aliya. One day, when this war is over, my Filipino wife and I will certainly visit Israel. For now, though, we are happy—as were the Jews of a previous generation—to stay here in the promised land of these welcoming Philippine shores.

HITLER ON LAZADA

It felt like someone had yanked out my kidneys.

Unable to sleep, I'd opened my cell phone to Facebook for an early morning browse. There was the usual array of unread news bits, posts from my friends, and ads for everything from lingerie to potatoes.

Then something popped up I never expected to see; a portrait of Adolf Hitler on the cover of his infamous 1925 book *Mein Kampf.* "Biggest sale of the year!" the ad proclaimed, only 666 pesos. And, just below it, sat an array of Nazi memorabilia complete with golden eagles, brown-shirted uniforms, and flags bearing enormous black swastikas.

I'm no fainting daisy. I understand that the book—in which the future German dictator first laid out his plans to annihilate the Jews of Europe in what would become the Holocaust—is a work of some historic interest. Still, the timing was curious, as was the price, which many consider a sign of the devil. Was that intentional, or a simple act of cultural ignorance?

Everywhere, antisemitism is breaking out. As Israel pursues its vital goal of wiping out the Islamic terrorist group, Hamas, responsible for the deliberate, unprovoked torture and murder of more than 1200 Israeli civilians, campuses and cities worldwide are erupting in protests calling for death to Israel and the Jews.

On November 5, 2023, a Jewish man carrying an Israeli flag was killed by a pro-Palestinian protestor near Los Angeles,

California. And I'm seeing daily posts from frightened Jewish friends and relatives wondering whether we're on the brink of another Holocaust.

Hardly the ideal time for Lazada—the Philippines' leading online retailer—to roll out its hot new line of antisemitic Nazi products. Do Filipinos not understand the horrific message that sends?

Curious to find out, I conducted a private poll at the dinner table last night. Seated with me were four Filipino relatives and a close family friend, including three college graduates and a bright high school senior. "Who here knows about Hitler?" I asked. "Have any of you heard of the Holocaust?"

To my utter astonishment, the only one who knew what I was talking about was an 11-year-old nephew who said he'd heard about it on YouTube.

Part of my shock, of course, comes from a knowledge of the special historic relationship between the Philippines and the Jews. This island nation, as I've attested before, was one of the few that welcomed victims fleeing slaughter during World War II. And its 1947 UN vote played a crucial role in establishing the modern State of Israel.

And yet some recent Filipino writing on the subject is truly appalling. "Yesterday's oppressed have become today's oppressors," columnist Randy David bellowed in the *Philippine Inquirer*, commenting on Israel's efforts to defend its citizenry by putting Hamas permanently out of commission. "We cannot, by our silence or neutrality, be complicit in this heinous crime."

Like so many others, David blindly points to the tragic loss of civilian life in the Gaza Strip. Which, of course, empowers and encourages Hamas' strategy of maximizing those heartbreaking deaths by using civilians as shields prevented from heeding Israel's warnings to flee. Would he have been equally outraged by the massive death toll in Manila when the Allies liberated it from the Japanese in 1944?

"Many were massacred in atrocities by Japanese troops," the *Los Angeles Times* has reported, "but many also were pulverized by US artillery barrages. Countless others were maimed, impoverished and traumatized." The final toll; at least 100,000 unarmed Filipino civilians—10% of the population—dead in the streets of a nearly flattened city.

I don't recall a huge public outcry against the Americans following that horrific event. Nor were there massive protests when the Allies bombed Berlin at the end of World War II; instead, they were hailed everywhere as conquering heroes. Why then this double standard whenever Jews are involved?

During a trip to Germany last year to help memorialize family members murdered in the Holocaust, I was impressed by the German penchant to teach and learn from history rather than sweep it under the rug. Unfortunately, that healthy impulse may now be jeopardized by a new upsurge of antisemitic sentiment fueled, in part, by massive immigration from the Middle East.

And yet I felt buoyed by another Facebook post on the recent 85th anniversary of *Kristallnacht*, the notorious night in 1938 that marked the Holocaust's beginning. *Nie Wieder Ist Jetzt!* read the slogan emblazoned in lights on Berlin's notorious Brandenburg Gate, the historic icon of Nazism.

The translation: *Never Again is Now.*

It's a notion I heartily endorse.

CAN AMERICA BE TRUSTED?

It's a painful question. Especially for an American who wants, more than anything, to take pride in his homeland.

But events, both recent and historic, have brought it to the fore. And the current situation in the Philippines makes the answer imperative: Can America's allies count on the alleged superpower to keep its promises?

Here's a hint: the country's history is not encouraging.

That history begins long ago, shortly after the nation's founding. From 1778 to 1871, the United States signed 368 treaties with various indigenous tribes across North America. All were based on the fundamental idea that each tribe constituted an independent nation with its own right to self-determination and rule. And that the land those Native Americans inhabited belonged completely and solely to them.

One of the great tragedies of US history is that virtually all of those promises were ultimately discarded. And that their early disposal may have helped shape a national character that, to some extent, survives today.

The Philippines first felt the smack of American disingenuousness around the turn of the 19th century when, by lying to Filipinos regarding its true intentions, the US replaced Spain as the country's colonial master. Then, a few years later, American soldiers massacred untold numbers of Moros in Southern Mindanao after promising to govern them in peace.

Such broken and unfulfilled promises have not always been willful. The United States, after all, spent several years and more than 58,000 of its own citizens' lives defending South Vietnam's independence, only to be defeated and expelled by a smaller but more effective guerilla force. Anyone alive during the 1975 evacuation of Saigon can surely remember the anguished cries of those seeking inclusion, thousands of whom ended up in the Philippines.

Which, of course, brings to mind a more recent debacle; the bungled 2021 withdrawal from Afghanistan, leaving more than 1,000 Americans and Afghani visa holders at the mercy of the Taliban.

And now the country seems to be backing away from yet another alliance once considered ironclad, namely that with Israel. After suffering a devastating surprise attack on October 7th by the radical terrorist group governing Gaza, Israel declared its intention to, finally and completely, destroy Hamas. Which wasn't surprising, given the terrorists' long-term goal—expressed both in actions and in words—of obliterating the Jewish state and its inhabitants from the face of the earth.

America's initial reaction was welcomed and expected: a reiteration of the nation's "unshakable" support for Israel, its closest and longest-standing ally in the Middle East. Ah, but then the political landscape changed. Pro-Palestinian protestors gathered on college campuses across the country, expressing their opposition to Hamas' defeat. Palestinians in certain areas considered key in the upcoming presidential election quickly joined the fray. And top advisors warned of a potential replay of the 1968 debacle in which protestors opposing the Vietnam War wreaked havoc at the Democratic National Convention.

So the unshakable support began to shake. The US administration unilaterally paused weapons shipments previously approved by Congress, leaving the Israelis to fend for themselves. Apparently, it seemed, Israel was allowed to fight as long as it didn't win. "By halting the shipment," Israeli commentator Amit Segal asserted in the *Wall Street Journal*, the US "is effectively sending Hamas the most potent weapon of all: hope."

So what does all this have to do with the Philippines? Just that the country is relying heavily on American support in its growing conflict with China over the West Philippine Sea. Don't get me wrong, I side with the Philippines. And, to his credit, President Bongbong Marcos has also elicited the support of other allies, including Japan, France, and Australia, to name just a few.

Still, given America's wobbly history of reliability in keeping promises to friends, one can't help but question its commitment today. Which for me, both as an American citizen and expat in the Philippines, is a source of grave concern.

History's big exception, of course—and probably the reason most Filipinos still feel some affection for America—is Gen. Douglas MacArthur's triumphantly fulfilled World War II promise that "I shall return." If, God forbid, it ever becomes necessary, I pray for a repeat of that noble bit of history.

ZAMBOANGA REIMAGINED

Hanging out at the mall.

That's how thousands of Zamboaguenos spend their weekends these days. You see them buying groceries or strolling along the corridors with children in tow. Often elderly men gather in groups to sip coffee while loudly discussing the news of the day.

The malls are so crowded that finding a place to park on Sunday afternoon is akin to navigating traffic at Los Angeles International Airport. But they do it because they can. And because most of the malls are brand-spanking new.

In fact, Zamboanga City's economy is the fastest growing on the Zamboanga Peninsula, according to the City Development Council. In 2023 it reached an all-time high of P139.47 billion, dramatically up from the pre-pandemic level of P125.05 billion. And much of that can be seen in the many malls opened since 2015.

Al Jacinto, a long-time friend I recently visited there after suppressing my long-held apprehensions, attributes Zamboanga's flowering abundance largely to the harmony achieved by the 2014 Bangsamoro peace agreement that provided the framework for what eventually became the Autonomous Region in Muslim Mindanao.

"Lots of Muslims came to Zamboanga from neighboring islands with money to invest," says Jacinto, a seasoned journalist who's spent decades covering the region for *The*

Manila Times and other newspapers. "Inevitably, the city grew."

Indeed, Zamboanga's population of nearly a million—an almost two percent increase since 2023—is nearly 40% Muslim, up from 30% when I first visited there more than two decades ago. My most vivid memory of that trip, as I've written before, is interviewing a woman in a house pierced by hundreds of bullet holes from a nearby shootout that had killed 30 Muslim rebels.

"My kids have never been here because they're too scared," explained Susan Camins Sanz, a Zamboanga native who'd returned to her hometown after 34 years in California where she'd raised a family. "This is my home. You can't let fear rule your life."

Fear had nonetheless inflicted major damage. Absent the tourism that once sustained the city, Zamboanga had become something of a ghost town in which residents kept their distance and the streets brimmed with beggars. As one of the few foreigners there in 2002, I stayed mostly at my hotel, closely watched by armed security guards. And always followed the advice of local protectors who warned me never to go out alone.

"When I visited Zamboanga City in the 1990s," an American friend recently told me, "it was as if it wasn't part of the Philippines." He doesn't visit any more, he said, because his Filipino wife won't let him. In fact, he'd like to make the trip, he says, but "if we were captured and beheaded, I'd die of shame for having so stupidly ignored everyone's advice and common sense."

Indeed, that "common sense" persists to this day. Waiting to board my flight at the airport two weeks ago, I ran into another foreigner who described my, uh, testicles as "big ones" upon discovering my destination. "I sure wouldn't go there," he confidently assured me.

But I went anyway and am extremely glad I did. Because what I saw can only be described as inspiring. A brand-new seaside boulevard teeming with street vendors selling halal food to people who'd probably never tried it. A pleasant array of women wearing hijabs among those with their hair blowing free. And dinners at Muslim-owned restaurants with nary a pork dish on the menu.

"The restaurants shut down during Ramadan," warned Jacinto, referring to the Muslim holy month set to start the following week.

My earlier visit to Zamboanga culminated in a *Los Angeles Times* piece chronicling the journey of 1,700 former Zamboaguenos returning from around the globe "to show the world that it's safe to go back [home]," an organizer had explained.

What he was trying to tell us then may finally be true now.

ODE TO A GOOD FRIEND

I woke up this morning to the kind of news no one wants to hear.

"My papa is gone," the message began, and immediately I knew that a piece of my world was gone too. It took a while, though, to fully comprehend just what a dear piece it was.

The message came from the daughter of Al Jacinto, a correspondent for *The Manila Times* and my friend of nearly 20 years. The man who called me brother, she informed me, had succumbed to cancer at age 59.

"Thank you so much for visiting my papa when he was still fighting," she wrote, referring to the last time I saw him. That was just three months ago in Zamboanga City, where he spent most of his life.

The visit reminded us both of how we first met there in 2005. I was on assignment for the *Los Angeles Times*, and Al was my photographer. Our most vivid shared recollection, as I've said, was interviewing a woman in a house pierced by the bullet holes of Muslim rebels. Al and I reminisced on that memory as he gave me a tour of the new modernized city in which he took pride.

My other vivid memory of those early days in Zambo was marrying a local woman, with Al as my best man. The marriage didn't last, but the friendship did. And so I can say without reservation that he was my first real Filipino friend.

Al was the consummate newsman. If there was something going on and he could get there, he would. Writing for *The Manila Times* or *The Mindanao Examiner,* which he owned and operated, he told his stories in clear, crisp tones. And if there were photos to get, he would get those too, even at the risk of his own life or limb. Once during an uprising in Zamboanga, Al told me, he got so close that a rebel bullet nipped his ear.

He was also the consummate family man. He had four children—two boys and two girls—all of whom he put through college on paths to noble professions. And he supported Maritess, his devoted wife of 32 years.

Al did all that by becoming the most disciplined and hard-working man I've ever known. As the monstrous cancer slowly enveloped him, he never gave up. In and out of the hospital, he posted periodic updates on Facebook, documenting his medical journey. Here's the last one, dated just days before his death:

"Admitted to Zamboanga Doctors' Hospital for a battery of lab tests ahead of my chemo. Chilled a lot of the past nights, on-and-off fever, body ache, weak and tired, headache. Need six blood donors for six units of platelets...Doctors are dealing with [that] now, hence my stay in the hospital is prolonged for several days. So it's work-from-hospital mode now..."

Probably the kindest thing Al ever did for me was recommend me to *The Manila Times,* which now carries this column. Thanks, brother, I hope you can hear me. About two weeks ago, Al posted a poem by Dr. M.A. Chaudhary, which I'd like to share:

You came naked,
You will go naked.
You arrived weak,
You will leave weak.
You came without money and things,

You will leave without money and things.

Your first bath? Someone washed you.

Your last bath? Someone will wash you.

This is life!!!

So why so much malice, so much envy, so much hate, so much resentment and so much selfishness?

BE KIND to everyone and do good deeds.

We have a limited time on Earth, don't waste it in uselessness.

Last Christmas, he gifted me with a magnificent *kris*, the iconic wavy sword of the Philippines representing bravery, honor, and the resilient spirit of these island people. I have mounted it on a wall of my house that I pass every day. From now until my dying breath, seeing that sword will remind me of Al.

POSTSCRIPT

ROASTED ALLIGATOR OR FRIED RATTLESNAKE?

I gave them fair warning.

"OK," I said, facing a bevy of Filipino in-laws, nephews, and nieces, "it's almost Thanksgiving. We have a family tradition here that everyone at the table must say why they're thankful."

There were murmurs all around from my Bisayan-speaking relatives.

"Oh yes," I added, almost as an afterthought, "and because it's an American holiday, it's got to be in English. I'm telling you early so that you can prepare."

Suddenly, the murmur flattened into a moan.

Which reminded me of my Filipino wife's first American Thanksgiving back in 2008. She had never *seen* a turkey, let alone cooked one. And so we bought a pre-cooked Thanksgiving dinner, complete with all the trappings, including, of course, the gigantic bird. Then, working together, somehow heated it to the right temperature and laid it out on our table for the best Thanksgiving ever. Because, like the pilgrims before us, we were celebrating a recent arrival on those brand-new frontier shores, namely *hers*.

"Gosh," she told me later, "I think Thanksgiving is my favorite holiday."

Ah, but now we live in the Philippines where many still languish in the *Thanksgivingless* dark. And so, we've made it our mission to spread a few rays of *Thanksgivingish* light.

To be sure, the job has proven challenging. The biggest problem, by far, has been locating one of those giant edible birds to grace our table each year. While perhaps that wouldn't be so difficult in Manila or Cebu, here in Northern Mindanao, it's nearly impossible. And so for the last several years we've settled for an alternate roasted animal at the center of our table, namely *lechon*, otherwise known as pig.

I know what you're thinking; what's so bad about that? It's practically the national dish, and delicious to boot! Which, of course, is abundantly true. But here's the thing: it doesn't feel like Thanksgiving. For an American like me accustomed to traditional roasted turkey on the fourth Thursday of each November, well, somehow it's just not the same.

A recent article in the *Wall Street Journal*, however, made me feel better. Some Americans, it seems, are tiring of turkey. "More hosts," the headline read, "opt for exotic meats this holiday."

Among those revolutionary dishes are antelope, camel, kangaroo, elk, squirrel, and bear. Also, ostrich, elk, python, and rattlesnake. But by far the most popular, the newspaper reports, is—wait for it—yes, smoked alligator wrapped in bacon!

The "mild taste and tender texture can't be beat," the *Journal* reports, attributing that opinion to Kimberly Darling, 40, a nurse anesthetist who lives near Chicago and spends her free time hunting alligators.

Suddenly roasted pig doesn't seem so strange.

And so, we ate it again at this year's family Thanksgiving dinner. Along with baked yam, sweet potatoes covered with pecan, macaroni and cheese, mashed potatoes with white chicken-flavored gravy, roasted chicken, green bean casserole, ube cake, tapioca fruit salad, frozen mango float covered with graham crackers, watermelon, wine, and cooked crab garnished with garlic.

I mean, sheesh, how much yummier can it get?

Then came the time for those mandatory confessions...er, declarations of thanks.

There was lots of hemming and hawing, mixed with long silences, nervous laughter, and furtive glances at notes compiled on cell phones. “I’m thankful for, um, my family, good health, good food, and good fortune,” declared one particularly courageous soul, carefully concentrating on her diction.

She pretty much spoke for all of us.

Finally, my turn came. “I’m also thankful for those things,” I averred. “Oh, and one more thing: I’m thankful to have survived these darkened skies.”

My greatest hope is that one day soon, the heavens will lighten.

ACKNOWLEDGMENTS

First, as always, I want to thank those—both named and unnamed—who allowed me into their lives long enough to provide material for these essays. Many are family members who had little choice, so let me mention some. To my dear and patient wife, Ivy, who has never complained about my daily obsession with pounding out words, nor flinched when our private lives became fodder for my pen. To my beautiful children, Isaac and Adira, who have sometimes suffered my short-tempered snubs when their need for attention collided with my need to work. On the professional front, I'd like to thank Cong Corrales, editor of the *Gold Star Daily,* where many of these essays originally appeared. Also to Dante Ang, who hired me for *The Manila Times,* where the column now resides under the wise tutelage of editors Tessa Carmencita Arriola and Iza Iglesias, who give it a deeply appreciated free rein. And a special heartfelt thanks to Al Jacinto, a fellow journalist and dear friend, who steered me towards *The Times* with a much-needed recommendation. Though Al sadly did not live to see this book's publication, I hope and believe he would be proud. Finally, thanks to my publicist, Patrick Bonales, who has stood by me through thick and thin, and to my editor, Adina Morgan, whose input greatly influenced the book's ultimate form.

ABOUT THE AUTHOR

David Haldane is an award-winning American journalist, author, and radio broadcaster known for his insightful, poignant, and entertaining books, essays and short fiction. A former staff writer for the *Los Angeles Times*, where he contributed to two Pulitzer Prize-winning stories, Haldane has published three previous books. Currently Haldane lives with his Filipino wife and two young children in Northern Mindanao, Philippines, where he writes a weekly column for *The Manila Times* called “Expat Eye” and contributes regularly to the newspaper's *Sunday Times Magazine*. When not writing, he can often be found relaxing with a mug of rum on his veranda overlooking the sea or, more likely, hustling the children to bed.

OTHER TITLES BY DAVID HALDANE

NOTE FROM DAVID HALDANE

Word-of-mouth is crucial for any author to succeed. If you enjoyed *Dark Skies*, please leave a review online—anywhere you are able. Even if it's just a sentence or two. It would make all the difference and would be very much appreciated.

Thanks!
David Haldane

www.ingramcontent.com/pod-product-compliance
Lightning Source LLC
Chambersburg PA
CBHW051224210726
48290CB00003B/795

* 9 7 8 1 6 8 5 1 3 5 9 6 6 *